J·E·S·U·S
HAS A
QUESTION
FOR YOU

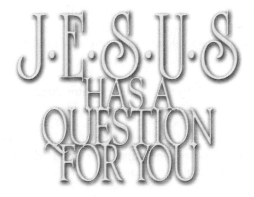

J·E·S·U·S HAS A QUESTION FOR YOU

Msgr. Richard C. Antall

Our Sunday Visitor Publishing Division
Our Sunday Visitor, Inc.
Huntington, Indiana 46750

For R. Justin Hennessey, O.P.
"Obsecro ut fiat duplex spiritus tuus in me."
("I pray you, let me inherit a double share
of your spirit." — 2 Kings 2:9)

TABLE OF CONTENTS

Question 17   89

And he sighed deeply in his spirit, and said, "Why does this generation seek a sign? Truly, I say to you, no sign shall be given to this generation." — Mark 8:12

Question 18   93

And being aware of it, Jesus said to them, "Why do you discuss the fact that you have no bread? Do you not yet perceive or understand? Are your hearts hardened? Having eyes do you not see, and having ears do you not hear? And do you not remember? When I broke the five loaves for the five thousand, how many baskets full of broken pieces did you take up?" They said to him, "Twelve." "And the seven for the four thousand, how many baskets full of broken pieces did you take up?" And they said to him, "Seven." And he said to them, "Do you not yet understand?" — Mark 8:17-21

Question 19   97

And when he had spit on his eyes and laid his hands upon him, he asked him, "Do you see anything?" — Mark 8:23

Question 20   100

And Jesus went on with his disciples, to the villages of Caesarea Philippi; and on the way he asked his disciples, "Who do men say that I am?" — Mark 8:27

Question 21   105

"But who do you say that I am?" Peter answered, "You are the Christ." And he charged them to tell no one about him. — Mark 8:29-30

Question 22   109

"For what does it profit a man, to gain the whole world and forfeit his life? For what can a man give in return for his life?" — Mark 8:36-37

Question 41   179

"How can the scribes say that the Christ is the son of David? David himself, inspired by the Holy Spirit, declared, / 'The Lord said to my Lord, / Sit at my right hand, / till I put thy enemies under thy feet.' / David himself calls him Lord; so how is he his son?" — Mark 12:35-37

Question 42   182

"Do you see these great buildings? There will not be left here one stone upon another, that will not be thrown down." — Mark 13:2

Question 43   186

"Let her alone; why do you trouble her?" — Mark 14:6

Question 44   190

"Simon, are you asleep? Could you not watch one hour?"
— Mark 14:37

Question 45   194

"Are you still sleeping and taking your rest?" — Mark 14:41

Question 46   197

"Have you come out as against a robber, with swords and clubs to capture me?" — Mark 14:48

Question 47   201

And at the ninth hour Jesus cried out with a loud voice, "Eloi, Eloi, lama sabachthani?" which means, "My God, my God, why hast thou forsaken me?" — Mark 15:34

I was teaching a Bible study to a small group of leaders in Intipuca, El Salvador. Every Friday night about twenty of us would meet in the church. The study had started as a response to a prayer group that had been veering toward fundamentalism. One of the leaders of the group had given me a book entitled *Discipleship* written by a Mexican priest.

The basic intent of the book was to make its readers meet Jesus in the Gospels and begin to imagine a personal discipleship. The style was simple, the editing made me think the work was self-published, and the main point was to have the student take the Bible in his hands and read it himself.

One chapter had several exercises for reading the Gospels. One of these was to look for the questions Jesus asks his disciples and other people in the Scripture texts. A complementary exercise was to read and reflect about the questions people put to Jesus in the New Testament. I decided that I would make a list of the questions and ask everyone in the class to react to them in imitation of the first suggested exercise in the book.

When I saw how many questions Jesus asks in the Gospels, I decided to narrow the field. Since St. Mark is the shortest Gospel, I thought I would just look at the questions of Jesus there. The bishops in El Salvador had ordered a special printing of St. Mark in a pamphlet form when it was the Marcan turn of the lectionary cycle. I wanted to read St. Mark with the group once we had steered clear of some of the problems obvious in the prayer group.

I was surprised to discover the number of questions that Jesus asks in the Gospel of St. Mark. It happens to be the Gospel with the most questions of Jesus.

It was an excellent study, and no one was bored. I did not go on and on as usual. My lectures had been a bit heady for the group, and I was paranoid about seeing eyes glaze over. The trick of the lesson worked. Everyone had a turn at reacting to the questions, which were very short texts but also very provocative ones. I asked each student which question of Jesus had the most resonance in his or her life. Many people chose different questions, which made things interesting.

I compared the other Gospels and found out that Mark's Jesus was, as we say in Spanish, a *preguntón*, somebody who asks an enormous number of questions. He asked rhetorical questions, he answered questions with questions (the "Irish" Jesus, I thought, thinking of my Celtic relatives), and he even died with a question on his lips. I didn't remember ever hearing that questions were a hallmark of Jesus' teaching in St. Mark, and I began canvassing my colleagues about the detail. They were impressed with the novelty of the approach, and began reflecting upon it. Asking questions was the divine prerogative, said one, remembering the climax of the book of Job, where God grills the poor impatient one with some of the most absurd rhetorical questions (my favorite is the one about the hippopotamus, which can be found in Job 40:15 in some translations).

I was very soon hooked on the subject. It could be a book, I thought: Jesus asks us the questions. Previous to my discovery, I had had a short list of other topics for books. Those ideas would have to wait. I had written two other books — I knew that I was started on another just because of what was going on in my head. I took a marker and highlighted the questions in my copy of the Navarre Bible's St. Mark. Then I wrote out each question in a notebook, one question per page. Under the English text, I wrote the Latin Vulgate as it appeared in the Navarre system, and then copied the Greek. I underlined key words and wrote out key ideas.

There was enough there for a book, I thought. Each question could be a starting point for a reflection. Such a book could be read straight through, or back to front, or dipped into according to taste. I would try to answer — or at least reflect on — the issue presented by each question. The first one I worked on was "My God, my God, why hast thou forsaken me?" (Mark 15:34), the last question in this book. Almost immediately, I recalled a woman whom I had met in my first parish. She had told me the story of her own brush with despair as she was crossing a huge old bridge over Cleveland's Cuyahoga River.

During the process of writing this book, many things have happened to me. I was transferred from Chirilagua to Puerto de La Libertad, the port city which is no longer a city but where I had worked from 1986 to 1993. This time I was to be pastor of a mixed international team and had been given the task of trying to leave the mission as soon as possible. As if this change were not traumatic enough ("Back to the Future," I had joked, because of all the emotion of returning to ministry where I had worked so long and hard), El Salvador suffered two severe earthquakes, which devastated the country, destroying thousands of homes and hundreds of churches. The aftershocks eventually totaled more than ten thousand. The personal reverberations of my change, and the new jobs I was given in the archdiocese, were perhaps of an equal number.

For two years, I kept chipping away at the questions. I wrote reflections early in the morning and sometimes late at night; I started writing them in Chirilagua and finished in La Libertad; I worked on them on vacation at home and while staying a Our Lady Chapel in downtown L.A. between stints preaching at churches in California, asking for money to rebuild Salvadoran churches and chapels. They were my mental baggage wherever I went; they were part of my prayer and my life. I scribbled in my notebook of questions when I read something

15

that I thought could be related to the theme, especially in my reading of St. Thomas's *Catena Aurea* commentary on the Gospels. Sometimes my notes were so inspired that I could not decipher them afterward. (Browning is said to have said of some obscure lines of poetry, "When I wrote these lines God and Browning knew what I wanted to say. Now only God does.")

At last I finished. I had a strange reaction to completing the project, a kind of postpartum blues. It took me much more effort than normal to write an introduction. I am now suddenly shy about the reflections that I have spent two years in writing and polishing. I don't know what that means in terms of your reaction to this book, but I guess it is an indication of the sincerity with which I wrote it. So here they are. I hope that they are at least as useful to you as points of departure for reflection and prayer as they have been for me.

God bless you for accompanying me. Good luck with the questions that Jesus asks you. ◇

"Why do you question thus in your hearts? Which is easier, to say to a paralytic, 'Your sins are forgiven,' or to say, 'Rise, take up your pallet and walk'?" — Mark 2:8-9

Jesus' ministry of preaching began after his baptism in the Jordan River and his retreat in the desert. According to the first chapter of St. Mark, he started with a kind of missionary journey throughout Galilee. After finishing this tour, he returned home to Capernaum, where his reputation had grown. News had spread fast about the wonders the Lord worked.

Thus it is easy to understand why there was a large group of people eager to hear his message when he arrived. In fact, so many people were in the house and its doorway that it was impossible to enter. One has to imagine the paralyzed man's carriers taking in the logistics of the situation. How to enter? The ingenuity shown in opening up the roof and letting the man down on ropes has to win our admiration. Certainly, it was something that arrested the attention of the crowd. What would Jesus do with this?

The miracle of the healing of the paralytic is subtly recalled by the architecture of the church of St. Peter in Capernaum in present-day Israel. The church is built on pillars over the ruins of what experts think is an ancient church and has a glass window in the floor. By looking down, one can see the ruins of the church, and the traces of an even older foundation of a house that many scholars believe to be St. Peter's. The building itself has the form of a ship in order to recall the Fisherman, but it actually reminded me of a UFO craft hovering over the ancient ruins. The structure allows one to share something of the point of view of the men who "went through the roof" to make contact with Jesus.

St. Mark implies that Jesus was impressed with the faith of those who brought the man to him. He "saw their faith," says the text, which makes us think about the opinion he might have about our faith. The faith of the men moved Jesus to say, "Child, your sins are forgiven of you," according to the literal Greek. The word for child is *teknon*, and is a key word in the New Testament, especially in St. John's writings, where they express Jesus' tender love for his disciples. There are thus two important notes about this greeting of Jesus: (1) the tender love he has for us, and (2) his power to forgive sins.

The scribes are offended by what Jesus has said. They consider his words blasphemy, because only God can forgive. Perhaps anyone who was there could sense the anger in the room. But Jesus could read hearts and so nothing at all was secret to him. He responded to the unspoken questions of the scribes with his own sense of surprise. "I'm surprised you're surprised" is often a disarming defense, and Jesus was an astute arguer. The heart of his argument with them, however, has to do with his power.

He says, "Which is easier to say?" and then gives the two options. Perhaps first we should talk about how different it is for Jesus to say something. His words have divine power. I could imagine, with the little respect for the truth that we have in modern-day America, that someone could respond to Jesus' question, "Why, both are easy to *say*." We say so much of what is not the truth. There is an Irish expression about the mendacious: "He says more than his prayers." There is a gap between saying and doing in our lives, however, that does not exist in the life of Jesus.

His word is the Hebrew *dabar*, the word of the Lord. It is efficacious, bringing about what it expresses, like the words of God in Genesis, "Let there be light." This passage of St. Mark is really about Jesus' divinity, and we can see that in three items. There is the efficacious divine word, then there is the power to forgive sins, and finally there is the healing of a paralytic.

The question "Which is easier?" recalls the questions that God puts to Job in their famous encounter. That "quiz" began with, "Who is this that darkens counsel by words without knowledge?" and then proceeds to inquire, "Where were you when I laid the foundation of the earth?" No wonder after the series of questions — which include "Have you commanded the morning since your days began?" and "Is it at your command that the eagle mounts up and makes his nest on high?" — Job answers humbly, "I lay my hand on my mouth" (Job 38:2, 38:4, 38:12, 39:27, 40:4).

An honest response to Jesus' question would be, "We cannot say which is easier, because both are impossible for us to say. We cannot forgive sins, and we cannot heal paralytics (at least not in our own names and if it is in Jesus' name, we are not healing, *he* is)."

The fact that we cannot really answer the question is the answer. Only Jesus is Lord. He is the only one capable of healing and forgiving us.

Were we in the crowd that day in Capernaum, we might have been hard put to answer this first of Jesus' questions in St. Mark. However, to our great fortune, we don't have to answer the question before he gives the answer. That is the advantage of following the story of the disciples in St. Mark. They make the mistakes, and we learn from them. It is as if the teacher is asking the same question of the whole class, and we get to hear the answers of others before it is our turn.

Theology means the study of God. That part of theology that concerns itself with Christ has a proper name: "Christology." This first question of Jesus in St. Mark leads us directly into a series of Christological issues. It talks to us about the powers of the Messiah (which is the Hebrew for the Greek

Christos, the Christ). Jesus was the Christ and therefore he could read men's hearts, could heal their infirmities, and could forgive their sins. Although Jesus first confronts us with a question, something that is not always pleasant in human encounters, we are led to conclude from the question many wonderful and consoling things.

Our reading of the questions of Jesus should help us relate to him more. A teacher who asks a great deal of questions in class is bound to get from those who don't want to speak, not only little eye contact, but also, perhaps, closer attention. We don't want to be caught off guard, or dreaming of other things. Jesus has many questions for us, and we can profit from all of them. From this first question we have learned about the divinity of Jesus expressed in healing love, a healing that reaches to the soul in the forgiveness of sins.

The lesson should stay with us. A concrete application is what can help us. We don't have to have friends lower us through the roof of the confessional in order to have access to God's mercy, although the company of friends in conversion is often critical. We know that we can approach Jesus in the sacraments for healing and forgiveness. He says to us, "Take up your pallet and walk." Those of us who have frequent access to the sacrament might be the walking wounded, but we are still ambulatory. That is because of Jesus' power. May we always believe in it. ◇

"Can the wedding guests fast while the bridegroom is with them?"   — Mark 2:19

Jesus is responding here to the people who wondered why his disciples did not fast like the followers of John the Baptist and the Pharisees. It is typical of Jesus to ask a question in response to a question. The answer to his question is the answer to their question. But Jesus' question requires a bit of explanation.

First of all, there is the wedding feast. Jesus uses the image of a wedding feast several times in the Gospels. One is the parable about the rich man's son's wedding feast, where the invited guests decline to come and are replaced by the poor and the sick. In St. John's Gospel, Jesus' first miracle takes place during a nuptial celebration. The abundance of the water changed to wine is a key to the transformation of the world by the grace of God offered in his Son.

Various aspects of the wedding customs of the time were very useful for Jesus in explaining his mission. The wedding was a celebration based upon invitation. Jesus' Good News was also an invitation. The key point in the ceremony was the arrival of the bridegroom at the house of the bride to take her home. In present-day America, it is usually the bride who keeps people waiting, but that wasn't the case in Palestine. That helps to express the idea of waiting for the arrival of the Messiah. When the bridegroom arrived, the rejoicing began. When the Messiah came, there was a new reality. The wedding imagery explains the difference between the Old Testament and the New Testament. Christ is the bridegroom who has been a long time in arriving.

The prophet Hosea in the Old Testament had described the relationship of God to his people in the strange image of a man marrying a prostitute and rehabilitating her. Sometimes I can understand why an old woman told me that she was disappointed in the Bible because it detailed so many sins. Marriage to prostitutes would hardly earn a G-rating even in Hollywood, and yet here it is in the word of God. The humiliation implied in marriage to a prostitute becomes in Hosea a tremendous metaphor of the love of God. The message is that God's love is all-forgiving and transforming.

Part of the book of the prophet Isaiah also uses the marital metaphor. "For your Maker is your husband, the LORD of hosts is his name; / and the Holy One of Israel is your Redeemer" (Isaiah 54:5). Jeremiah also refers to the early relationship of Israel with the Lord in terms of spousal love: "I remember the devotion of your youth, / your love as a bride, / how you followed me in the wilderness, / in a land not sown" (Jeremiah 2:2). Ezekiel also has a long treatment (chapter 16) of a man's marriage to an unfaithful wife as an allegory of the love of God for Israel.

Jesus' use of wedding imagery had to make those who knew the Scriptures think about Hosea, Jeremiah, Isaiah, and Ezekiel. "Scripture is the word of God that bears witness to God's Word [that is, Jesus]," said the great Swiss theologian Hans Urs von Balthasar. The marriage imagery of the prophets was a series of advance notices of the Eternal Bridegroom. In Jesus we have the definitive wedding of God's love and human destiny. So many elements we associate with weddings even now — a new beginning, tender love, and a source of celebration — connect easily with our understanding of the difference Jesus makes in our lives.

Mystics have elaborated very much on this spousal imagery but in ways that often seem strange to modern ears. C. S. Lewis mentions that it gave him pause at an early stage of his conversion, and we can understand his confusion about the comparison of divine love with human spousal love. St. Catherine of Siena used a quite graphic image to indicate that she regarded herself as a "bride of Christ." Some male mystics used the spousal imagery applied to the soul, which was considered feminine for metaphoric purposes.

But Jesus' interest here seems to be in the wedding guests more than in the bride or other details of the espousal. The Greek, which we have translated here as "wedding guests," translates, literally, "the sons of the bridal chamber." This is a direct translation of the Hebrew and was the name for the attendants of the groom. Jesus is thus commenting upon his closeness with the disciples. They are like the young friends of the bridegroom, sharing in a special way his joy. It is their privilege not to fast, at least *for the time being.*

That is the menace behind the adverb *while.* The clear implication is that they would fast later. While in other places the wedding banquet appears to be an image of the eternal happiness of heaven, here it is signaling the special time when Jesus' presence was palpable and did not require faith. The First Letter of St. John reveals the blessing of the apostles, "which we have heard, which we have seen with our eyes, which we have looked upon and touched with our hands" (1 John 1:1). The wedding ceremony would not last forever, although the marriage of grace and destiny was eternal. Far off on the horizon, Jesus pointed to a cloud perhaps no bigger than the palm of a man's hand but one that promised storm.

If we were to answer the question of Jesus as it stands, we would not hesitate to say, "Of course, the wedding guests should not fast while the groom is still with them." However, I wonder if it is as obvious to us that there is a second interrogative hidden in this question. What should the wedding guests do when the groom has gone away? Is it not the time to fast?

For most of us, fasting has been reduced to two days a year, Ash Wednesday and Good Friday, although the Church also recommends that Holy Saturday before the vigil be considered special as well. Few Catholics fast, and those who don't are inclined to think of it as an activity that is suspiciously fanatic, or at least special. The implication of this question is the contrary. So is the tradition of holiness in the Church.

Penance is a natural part of the life of the Christian. When I was growing up, this was still seen in the Friday abstinence from meat. I remember once staring at some grilled hot dogs that my Protestant relatives were eating on a Friday, and I couldn't figure out why they had bought me a fish sandwich. Then an aunt, perhaps because of my roving eyes at the table, asked why I didn't have a hot dog. Another relative replied, "It's Friday — they can't eat meat." I was perhaps ten years old but felt as though I had escaped a threat on my life. I had been thinking of asking for the hot dog. What kind of Catholic would they have thought me, I wondered? Thank God, I had said nothing.

The experience is funny but points out a reality that some other North American Catholics have missed with the decline of the Friday abstinence. It was a reminder to sacrifice in some way every week. Part of the reason the Church changed the law was the fact that many Catholics did not eat meat every day anyway, and the abstinence hardly achieved its purpose. However, Pope Paul VI, who relaxed the law of abstinence, asked for Catholics to continue to do penance every Friday. It would be easier for most of us to maintain the abstinence as a reminder of the sufferings of Jesus on Good Friday than to search out special penitential practices.

Fasting is a spiritual activity based on physical sacrifice. If one looks to the history of the Church and the lives of the saints, fasting and other types of penance were constant companions of the life of the Spirit. Many saints saw fasting as a special weapon against temptations involving chastity. The irony of our age is that the most extreme diets are accepted as personal achievement, but fasting is regarded with suspicion. If you are fasting because of vanity, the world applauds you. When it is part of a program of prayer or penance, people wonder if you are all there. Abstinence from meat on Friday might be considered old school, but houses that have banned red meat from the table are abundant.

Part of the reason we need to read the Scriptures is to give ourselves a perspective that can defy commonly accepted opinion. This question of Jesus in our context leads me to think about how little I do to sacrifice outside of the time of Lent. The bridegroom is in heaven, and we await his return. Our sacrifices witness to our waiting and remind us that our lives are not yet complete.

The questions of Jesus can provoke responses in us if we have the imagination to not just overhear them but to listen to them as if they were directed at ourselves. Those who asked Jesus the question about his disciples' fasting were presumably trying to insinuate a criticism about him. We know that he later remarked that some had accused him of being a glutton because he did not have the same diet as St. John the Baptist. I think that we should consider how others might reject Jesus because of the discipleship we live. Might others not say, "Do these people really believe in sacrifice when they practice it so little?" ◇

"Have you never read what David did, when he was in need and hungry, he and those who were with him: how he entered the house of God, when Abiathar was high priest, and ate the bread of the Presence, which it is not lawful for any but the priests to eat, and also gave it to those who were with him?"

— Mark 2:25-26

Did you know about the story of David, and his eating the bread of the Presence? The question presumes some knowledge of the Old Testament, and many Christians today have only the vaguest notions of the stories and figures from that part of the Bible. Who was David? When was he "in need"? Who were with him in his necessity? What is meant by the house of God, given that there was no Temple in the time of David? What was the bread of the Presence? Why did David break the law? Why does Jesus see this example as the answer to those who criticize the disciples, saying, "Why are they doing what is not lawful on the sabbath?" (Mark 2:24).

Perhaps the most important point for anyone reading this passage is to understand the relationship between the Old Testament and the New. Anyone who studies the Bible is confronted with its division in two parts, the first about the promise of salvation and the second about its fulfillment, as a hymn in Spanish has it. The Old Testament reflects the Old Covenant and its history — you could even say its prehistory — in the accounts of Creation and the Fall. The New Testament conveys the New Covenant between God and man that is realized in Jesus Christ, Son of God and Savior of humanity.

The New Testament provides the basis of understanding the Old Testament, however, and not necessarily vice versa. The Bible is the word of God about the Word of God, Jesus the Christ. This principle, expressed by Hans Urs von Balthasar, is the Christian key to the Scriptures. Even the Old Testament is about Jesus, the definitive Word of God. The Christian cannot read the Old Testament merely as the Jewish Scriptures, as some biblical criticism taught even in seminaries would have it.

The word of God in both Testaments is the special possession of the Church and also in a way her product. There can be no doubt about which came first, the Bible or the Church, like the famous puzzle of the chicken or the egg. The Church existed before the entire Bible was written down. If not, how could some of the letters of the New Testament be addressed to Christian communities? The Bible cannot be somehow separated from the Church and her history.

The Protestants failed to understand this principle when they cut certain books out of the Bible, even though they had been accepted by Christians for many centuries. Instead of following the tradition of the Church, the Protestant Reformers decided that the Pharisees at Jamnia in Palestine in the year 90 were the authority on the Old Testament. These same "authorities" rejected all of the New Testament. Why were the rabbis more important than the Fathers of the Church in determining the contents of the word of God? Rejecting the authority of the Roman Catholic Church, the Protestants gave their vote to the Pharisees. The Old Testament also is about Christ.

There has been a more recent reflection of misunderstanding the essential relationship between the Old Testament and the New in the controversy some years back about the bishops' sponsored translation of the psalms. This translation was rejected by the Vatican because it had sacrificed linguistic exactitude on the altar of political correctness. Some theologians were upset because the gender-free translation eliminated any Christological reading of the psalm. The translators weeded out the word "man" and put several awkward substitutes for it in each place of use (my favorite substitute was "mortals," which makes me think of something out of Anne Rice). This was done so that the substantive nouns could be "all-inclusive." The trouble is that the elimination of the word "man" sometimes made all interpretation in terms of Christ impossible. In fact, the new translation required a discrepancy for political correctness's sake between a psalm and its translation in the New Testament.

New Testament understanding of the Old Testament starts with Jesus. In this question we are studying, he is arguing like a rabbi with the rabbis, proof text counter proof text. Your disciples are violating the Sabbath laws by plucking the ears of grain as they walked through the fields. This activity was not stealing, because anyone hungry could do this; the problem was that they did it on the Sabbath. Jesus answers his critics by saying that David violated the law about the bread of the Presence because of his hunger. One case answers another, and Jesus proves that David himself violated the law because of necessity.

There are other things here that we can appreciate also. The Son of David (this was a title of the Messiah) refers to David. Both had enemies: Jesus is criticized by the Pharisees; David is fleeing Saul. The followers of Jesus are hungry, as are David's soldiers. There is another element beyond the parallels between Jesus and David. The bread of the Presence is recalled by the Bread of Life. The twelve loaves (for the twelve tribes) offered in front of the Ark of the Covenant in its tabernacle were an offering to the Lord that prefigured the Eucharist in a way. Hearing Jesus talk about the loaves should start us making connections.

That is why we can get two important ideas from this question of Jesus. Not only do we see that he wanted us to understand that the Son of man was Lord of the Sabbath, but also he showed us how the Old Testament continues in the New. This is by no means easy. There are elements of the Old Testament that can be confusing. In this case, there seems to be a printer's error in St. Mark: Abiathar was the son of the high priest Ahimelech, who gave David the bread. The "house of God" referred to was the tent of the Ark of the Covenant, which was considered the dwelling place of the Divine Presence. These are details, however, and familiarity brings facility to Bible study.

"Have you not read?" is addressed to us as well. This question of Jesus can be a challenge to us to read the Old Testament. We can start by reading 1 Samuel 21:1-9. ◇

"Is it lawful on the sabbath to do good or to do harm, to save life or to kill?"   — Mark 3:4

In Logic class, the dilemma offered by this question would be called a *reduction ad absurdum*, the reduction of an idea to absurdity. Who could say, "It is lawful to do harm, or to kill"? There is no option about answering the question. Jesus evidently wants to show that his opponents have taken an absurd position. They have put "doing good" as contrary to religion.

In St. Mark, this confrontation in the synagogue is crucial in explaining what happened to Jesus. This Gospel is so short that the narrative sweeps us along sometimes, and we do not give due weight to everything said because it is said so succinctly. It is worthwhile taking a moment to look at the scene closely. The evangelist is providing here the who-what-where-why-when of the plot against Jesus' life.

Who? "They" were waiting and watching, says the Gospel, to see what he would do. William Barclay interprets these men to be inquisitors sent out by the Sanhedrin to investigate the Galilean preacher who was attracting so much attention. The text says that they were Pharisees, and it looks like this group was cohesive enough to decide to make a united front against Jesus.

Jesus was well aware that he was under surveillance by the "religious" authorities. That is clear from the way he deliberately provokes the Pharisees by saying, "to save life or to kill," a phrase that goes even beyond the dilemma of "to do good or to do harm." The short scene in which this question appears has a violent background. Jesus asks about whether it is right to kill, perhaps because his opponents were thinking of killing him, as the text confirms a little further along.

What? The reason for the decisive break with the Pharisees is the cure of the man with the withered hand on the Sabbath. I live in a rural section of a poor country. When an accident happens that causes someone to lose the use of his hand, it is a tragedy that affects family life. That is why I have no trouble seeing this man in my mind and understanding the remarkable grace of Jesus' cure. There is a sort of legend about this man, perhaps depending upon the fact that the Greek word used to describe his infirmity implies that the hand had not been withered at birth. The apocryphal Gospel of the Hebrews has it that he was a stone mason. Jesus was perhaps literally "saving the man's life" because he earned his daily bread by his hands.

The reader of St. Mark must ask, "What could possibly be wrong with curing the man?" The problem was an understanding of religion that did not see the call to fraternity as the most important measure of faith. The Pharisees, who thought more of the externals of religion than of compassion for the suffering, echoed Cain's question, "Am I my brother's keeper?" This man's problem should not impinge upon our Sabbath. In other words, "his tragedy has nothing to do with my religion." This is the contrast between the religion of laws and the religion of love. I fulfill the law and I save myself because I follow the rules. Love makes many rules superfluous, not because it is against the law but because it goes beyond it.

When? St. Mark presents this confrontation fairly early in the ministry. "That was the beginning of the end, that healing in the synagogue," is what he is saying. It is common among us in analyzing things as diverse as falling in love and breaking off with people to try to trace changes to a point of origin. In St. Mark, this is the point of no return for Jesus. "Here he crossed the Rubicon," it says. There was something inevitable about his death once the Herodians and the Pharisees, who had been enemies, had concluded a pact against him.

Where? Jesus had continued to preach in the synagogues, even though, as the Bible scholar William Barclay says, that made the clashes with authority more likely. The synagogue was a place of prayer but not of sacrifice. Only in the Temple did priests offer the varied sacrifices required by the law of the Old Testament on the altar. In the synagogue there could only be the recitation of prayers and the study of the Torah and the prophets. The men who studied, however, were always hungry for other points of view. A visitor could give the synagogue instruction, an opportunity for evangelization that St. Paul never seems to have passed up when on his missionary journeys.

Why? When Jesus showed himself Lord of the Sabbath by working this miracle, he made inevitable the opposition of the Pharisees. Not only was he showing that religion was about love, not rules, but he also was indicating that God was not some kind of scorekeeper in the sky but close to us and compassionate. The Pharisees rejected both notions. They did not want a God who came so close.

How? That is a question I am not able to answer. Miracles seem to be suspensions of the laws of Nature to us. Perhaps they represent rather the fulfillment of the healing possibilities the Lord has built into his creation. At any rate, they remind us that our understanding is as limited as our powers. As Hamlet said to his friend, "There are more things in heaven and earth, Horatio, than are dreamt of in your philosophy." The power of Jesus to heal was one of the signs by which he taught the kingdom and demonstrated that he was the Messiah. It was the fulfilling of his mission that put him on a collision course with the powers that were.

We can see how this miracle was key to Jesus' ministry. What does his question have to teach us? Rhetorical questions are usually so obvious that it is not necessary to go to great lengths to explain them. However, this rhetorical question of Jesus shows us the dynamics of his ministry in a few words. He was forced even to ask if doing good was permitted on the day dedicated to God. The obtuseness of the Pharisees made the question necessary. And presently, they did evil on the Sabbath, planning the death of Jesus.

But this is still disconnected from us, because we can say *they* rejected Jesus, a long time ago. The question can be current also. We can ask ourselves if we are not in danger, sometimes, of doing what the Pharisees did, to quote Shakespeare from the same play as above, "With devotion's visage / And pious action we do sugar o'er / The devil himself."

It is a cherished cliché of the modern spirit that religion actually makes one less charitable. I certainly do not want to give further credence to that canard; it does pain me to see how many people who wear their religion on their sleeves, so to speak, display little charity for others. When I worked with migrant workers in the States, I made the bitter discovery that the leaven of the Pharisees did not disappear in New Testament times. There were people who wondered why the Church had to worry about the poor who were far from their homes and "strangers in a strange land." Why did these people come here illegally? Why did they insist on speaking their own language? Why were they different from the rest of us?

It is more than two years after I left that parish that I write this. I made many friends there, and I am sure many good people just could not understand me as I cannot understand them. However, there are moments when I feel almost overwhelmed by the emotions that surface for me when I remember the opposition to the ministry I had to the immigrants. I am confused at times by those emotions, and sometimes angry. But the worst of it is that I am hurt by some memories, and don't know what to do with that hurt. I am much more comfortable being angry, as many who know me would be glad to assure you. That is why, even as I write this, I am surprised by what I am feeling. It is as if I am taking off a bandage on a wound I refused to look at.

I don't pretend to accuse the people who could not accept the Mexicans in my parish of being Pharisees. No doubt it would take more than a few pages to write about my mistakes. I was sent by the bishop to work with the migrants, I said so verbally and by the apportionment of my time and energy. However, the concept was too hard for some people. I remember that a woman said during my time at the parish, "I wish my kids spoke Spanish so that Father would take an interest in them." She was hurting no doubt, but I was too hurt at the idea that someone could not understand what I was trying to do to get past the jealousy that would rob the poor of my pastoral care. The other people had two priests to take care of them.

This question led me down a personal path, which I have imposed on you, the reader. However, it can be a model of how to take these questions of Jesus. My own question — "Why can't you let me do what I was sent to do?" — can hardly compare to Jesus' asking whether it was possible to do good on the Sabbath. However, it echoes what I think is implicit in Jesus' question. Couldn't they let him help? Were they so blinded by hate? Couldn't they see his love for them? I am sure that most people, if they dig deep enough into their experience, could come up with some experiences similar to mine, of frustration in wanting to do good. Perhaps that is the way we can use this question to get closer to Jesus. ◇

"How can Satan cast out Satan?" — Mark 3:23

More inquisitors had come from Jerusalem to investigate Jesus. They could not deny the truth of the many exorcisms attributed to Jesus, and so they declared that this preacher cast out demons by the power of "Beelzebul." This was the way the Jews talked about the devil, mispronouncing the name of a Canaanite deity (and sometimes changing the name to Beelzebub, which means "Lord of the Flies"). Jesus became aware of their criticisms (we can imagine somebody running from one group to another to spread the news). He calls them over to speak with them. This gives Jesus the higher ground immediately. The inquisitors are called to the inquest.

Very typically, Jesus answers their charges with a question that invalidates their argument. If Jesus is working for Satan, the devil must be working against himself. It is the logical gambit of *reductio ad absurdum*, reducing the opponent's premise to something illogical and absurd.

For some modern sensibilities, it is worth noticing that Jesus does not doubt the existence of Satan, nor the antagonism between Beelzebul and God. Some people today think that some Christians are so impressed with the forces of the opposition that they discount the power of God. Supposedly such types are dualists, whose world resembles that described by the Manichean heresy, which saw two gods, one good and one bad, at work in creation.

Perhaps more dangerous than the dualists are those who deny the personal character of evil. C. S. Lewis, in *The Screwtape Letters*, has the demons joking about the advantages of making people doubt their existence. If someone naïvely discounts the personal force of evil in the world, he is likely to have his defenses down when Satan comes calling.

This reminds me of a discussion at a priests' meeting in El Salvador. The theme of the session was the power of evil and how to discuss this in an evangelization retreat. A European missionary, formerly a chaplain to the Marxist guerrillas and now reinstated in the diocesan clergy, raised his hand and had a quizzical expression on his face. Wasn't all this discussion a bit much? Did we really think that the power of evil was personal? Certainly there is resistance to good in the world, but that came from people.

Practically no one there understood his point. None of the native priests would ever question the "personal" nature of the devil. Evil exists in our hearts, and is very often more than just "resistance" to the good. But there is also a force for evil in the world, in eternal enmity with God. They looked at the priest, who was reflecting a modern — or rather modernist — theological sensibility, as though he were speaking another language. Ironically, one old priest, who had been very much opposed to the guerrillas, was quick to understand that the European priest doubted the existence of the devil.

"He says that because he has made a pact with the devil," he said in a stage whisper. It can help you understand something about El Salvador to let you know that everyone laughed, including the two principals involved. The civil war, which tore apart the country for twelve years, did not leave it bereft of humor. The bishop quickly intervened to say that believing in the existence of the devil was doctrine and not a theological option. The speaker went on about the reality of evil and the necessity of choosing the good.

I have some trouble believing in stories about people selling their souls to the devil, although El Salvador has legends to that effect for every rich family in the country. Nevertheless, I felt much closer to the old priest's view of the world than that of the younger (although older than I) ex-guerilla chaplain. Christian revelation insists upon a personal force for evil from Genesis to Revelation.

Jesus was very clear about the opposition of the devil to God's plan, and his temptation in the desert can be seen as schematic of his ministry — a contest of wills between the Savior and Satan. The "ruler of this world" (John 14:30, 16:11) was his antagonist who started by trying to buy him out by offering comfort for the flesh and worldly glory. Jesus' ministry was the tenacious wresting the world from the dominion of Satan, which is something the exorcisms of St. Mark's Gospel should help us to see. Eventually (and inevitably) Jesus had to shed his blood to liberate us. That should make us take the Opposition seriously.

Jesus evidently did. That is why he objects to the enormity of the accusation making him an accomplice of Satan. We should react to the charge similarly. If our actions are sometimes judged by others unfairly, we can look to this example for comfort. They accused the One who was freeing the world from the power of Satan of really being a part of the corruption. The Holiest of the Holy was accused of serving the Worst of the Worst. Surely our petty grievances cannot compare to the enormity of accusing the Good of being Badness itself.

There is an implicit question behind Jesus' question, and that is about which side we are on in the conflict between the Redeemer and the Head Jailer of the human spirit. If, like Jesus and his opponents, we accept the cosmic antagonism between good and evil, then we have to decide on which team we will play, because even the audience is pulled into this game of all games. There are no sidelines on which to sit in the game of salvation, since everyone is a player.

In the *Spiritual Exercises* of St. Ignatius there is a famous meditation that proposes the vision of two armies arrayed on a field of battle. Ignatius' title was, "Meditation on the two banners, one Christ's, our chief Captain and Lord, and the other of Lucifer, the mortal enemy of our human nature." The person doing the *Exercises* must imagine choosing between the two battle lines. Whose side is he on? Which flag will he follow? Where will he stake his life?

The concept of life as a struggle between good and evil is not necessarily natural to us. Cardinal Carlo María Martini, in a reflection on the Ignatian meditation, said that much of our frustration with life is that we expect things to evolve steadily toward the good. "Thus we forget," said the cardinal, "that the daily life of the Christian is a constant struggle against the suggestive power of idols, against Satan and his effort to lead man to incredulity, desperation, and moral and physical suicide." This is not about some kind of souped-up ghost story, like the movie *The Exorcist*, but the persistent and subtle work of a being more intelligent than we are, and capable of taking infinite pains to create an atmosphere of pressure against the good.

Life as spiritual combat does not always harmonize with modern (or modernist) sensibility. Perhaps that is why the Church asks not only whether we reject Satan but also all his works and seductions in the baptismal promises and their renewals. It is possible that we might not like Satan at all but be on rather friendly terms with some of his works or especially with some of his seductions. We need a vision of Christ, wrote Cardinal Martini, "as a leader in the battle of life who is always comforting and giving us new courage and who knows how hard the struggle is, and long, and how merciless and astute the enemy is." Some of us forget sometimes that we are in a battle.

This question has given us a view of the world in only a phrase. How does it relate to your view of the world? The antagonism between good and evil is played out in your life, even if you are unaware of it sometimes. The saints — and, of course, Jesus — never lost a consciousness of the wars of the spirit. Maybe you could profit from seeing your soul as a corner of the battlefield. ◇

"Who are my mother and my brethren?"   — Mark 3:33

Jesus gave the answer to this question, which makes it unusual, perhaps unusually important. "And looking around on those who sat about him, he said, 'Here are my mother and my brethren! Whoever does the will of God is my brother, and sister, and mother' " (Mark 3:34).

The community of Jesus is defined by this answer in two directions. The common ground is doing the will of God, and this makes a special kind of family. Jesus seems almost to throw the predicates at whoever does the will of God, "brother, and sister, and mother." It is significant that he does not use the word "father." That would have been to prejudice one of his key insights, "God is Father." There are some people who are uncomfortable with what they call the "patriarchal" connotations of God as Father, and resent even the use of the masculine possessive pronoun when applied to God (hence barbarisms such as "God and God's people" to avoid the simpler "his"). Their problem on its deepest level is with one of the essential points of Jesus' teaching, God who is "Abba, Father."

As disciples, we are invited to reflect immediately on the new family Jesus is talking about here. His *family* transcends the family we ordinarily think about. Those who were present received in that look around the room an incredible privilege. In his eyes, they were intimately related to him. I reflect about this when I am celebrating the Eucharist sometimes. I look at the variety of people in the church, sometimes remembering their special trials and problems, and I think, "You are brother, sister, mother, to me."

This does not deny the nuclear family but certainly transcends it. If Jesus asked a Sunday congregation, "Who are my mother and my brethren?" I am sure that most would come up with the answer, "We are." However, there is a great gap between saying that the community of the Church is based upon seeking the will of God and that other disciples are my family and really living those beliefs. What a radical change it would mean for all our parishes if we took seriously what Jesus was saying in his house in Capernaum surrounded by his disciples.

Perhaps the difficulty of this teaching explains why so many have been distracted from the message of Jesus to the circumstances surrounding the question. The text says that "his mother and his brethren" had come to Capernaum. No doubt this is connected with the plot to destroy Jesus that we have seen in connection with Question 4 of this work.

Naturally, there is a question: Who were these brethren of Jesus? Catholics believe in the doctrine of the perpetual virginity of Mary. That means that the Blessed Virgin Mary did not have other children. Although even Luther seems to have accepted the perpetual virginity of Mary, in general the congregations born of the Protestant Reformation insist on a literal and limited understanding of the "brethren" referred to in this verse and in Mark 6:3.

The Greek word used is *adelphoi*, which is "brothers" certainly, although often given a much wider significance than what we would translate merely as "siblings." In fact, the majority of references to *adelphos* (the singular Greek form) uses the word in a metaphoric way. In the Sermon on the Mount in Matthew 7:3-5, Jesus asks why we are preoccupied with "the speck . . . in your brother's eye" and not in the plank in our own. Obviously, he is using "brother" for "neighbor" here.

The Old Testament, following Semitic usage and custom, called relatives we would call nephews and cousins, "brothers." An example of this wider sense of the word is found in at least one translation of Genesis 13:8, where Abraham says to his nephew Lot that they are "brothers." The New Testament does not make distinctions that are common in English, like half-brother or half-sister, to describe a sibling who shares only one parent.

The Church has always insisted that the so-called "brothers and sisters" of Jesus were not children of Mary, although some Fathers of the Church, including Jerome, have talked about the possibility that they were children of Joseph by a previous marriage. The hypothesis that Joseph was a widower fit well with the assumption that he was much older than Mary, something that is still echoed in images and holy cards of St. Joseph.

In El Salvador, we often hear about the issue of the family of Jesus from fundamentalists who try to confuse Catholics by saying that Mary did not remain a virgin. My answer to questions about this is to detail how "brothers and sisters" are given a wide sense in common usage in El Salvador. First cousins are called *primos hermanos* in Spanish, which literally translated means "cousins-brothers." Many people identify others who are raised with them as *hermanos*, even if they are not blood relatives. *Hermano de crianza* is the term used for siblings by a sort of adoption.

Not too long ago, on All Souls' Day, I ran into an example of this. A young woman asked me for a ride after a Mass in a cemetery. She told me that she lived in another town but had gone to the cemetery to put flowers on the grave of her "sister." She had walked an hour to where she could catch the bus to go to the place, because otherwise "no one would decorate" her "sister's" grave. Her "sister" was someone who had been "given" to her mother. Children who are *regalados* (which means "given as a gift") are a tradition here in El Salvador. "Brothers and sisters" are elastic terms in the States because of the reality of divorce and remarriage (my father's family was an example of this), but in El Salvador there is an even more common extension of meaning.

Besides the "extended" family experience, it is frequent in El Salvador for people to say "brother" to fellow members of a congregation. This is almost universal among Protestants but also common among Catholics in certain movements. All of this makes the metaphoric use of "brethren" easy to understand. For many, the crowning argument of Mary's perpetual virginity comes from St. John's Gospel. If Jesus had siblings, why would he entrust his mother to one of his disciples? As strict logic, this is not compelling (siblings sometimes fight and children and parents disown each other); but in a society that still holds for the responsibility that children have for their parents, it indicates that Mary was with Jesus because there was no other place she could be. It is an insight based upon identification: "What else would she do as a widow?"

Ultimately, our faith in the Church has to be decisive. As I tell the people who question me here, the Church did not have to deduce Mary's perpetual virginity from biblical references — she *remembered* it. The same Church that tells me that the Bible is the word of God tells me how to interpret its message. The "discovery" that Jesus supposedly had siblings was made centuries after the Church had confirmed that the "brothers and sisters" of the Lord were not children of Mary. The word of God was not a message in a bottle, misunderstood until the Reformers appeared to argue their sometimes-conflicting versions of Christianity. The Holy Spirit was always with the Church, confirming the promise of Jesus never to leave us abandoned and always guaranteeing the truth of Tradition.

This is all a side issue, however, in terms of this question. The really important message of Jesus is that we are his brothers and sisters, that we are "mother" to him. What can this last mean? I think that it indicates the depth of intimacy to which he invites us. The relationship we have with our mothers is often so special because it involves a sense of shared existence. It is as if the connection we had with their lives in their wombs continues in some spiritual way. Jesus is offering us that kind of identity with him, that kind of connection.

Of course nowadays it is hard to find a reference to family that does not include with it the word "dysfunctional." There was a cartoon showing a man sitting alone in an auditorium, a sea of empty seats around him. Above the stage was a sign indicating that the event was a reunion of "children of functional families." Problems abound in all families, of course. Family intimacy is a great good, and good things are often subject to corruption in this world. There is a saying in Latin that tells us that "the corruption of the good is the worst." The comic who used to say, "We get along like brothers, like Cain and Abel," was expressing a bitter truth. From the beginning of salvation history, family has been a somewhat ambiguous reality, and so are metaphors related to it.

Jesus is talking about an unambiguous reality, however, which is doing the will of God. That is the basis of the vision of community implied by this question. Although we all have a tendency to seek community, at times we do not seek what is the basis of that community with the same dedication. We all want acceptance and togetherness, which are key ideas in the relationship Jesus talks about. We desire the permanence and the peace that we intuitively associate with the nonsexual intimacy and commitment expressed in the comparison with "brothers, sisters, and mother." However, we must ask ourselves about our commitment to seeking God's will.

The Protestant pastor Dietrich Bonhoeffer coined the famous phrase "cheap grace" to talk about a misunderstanding of God's love as something that did not demand our participation, the "cost of discipleship." There are many visions of shared community around that talk about being as intimate as brothers and sisters without establishing the strict connection with the will of God. These are false communities offering a cheapened concept of the union of disciples with Christ. True intimacy with the Lord is connected with true intimacy with one another and is also connected to doing the will of God. "In His will is our peace," taught the poet Dante, and so is the peace we share with one another.

My answer to this question of Jesus has to have three parts, therefore. One part is about my feeling of sharing intimately in Christ's life: I am family to him. Another is whether that intimacy is really shared by me with fellow disciples: They, too, are family to him and therefore connected to me. Finally, but also in the first place, I have to answer whether I am seeking to do God's will. I heard a child make a mistake once when learning the Our Father. He said, "*My* will be done on earth as it is in heaven." I have made the same mistake in my prayer and it hasn't been because I was tongue-tied but because I failed to think of God's plan first.

What do you say to this question of Jesus? ◇

"Do you not understand the parable? How then will you understand all the parables?" — Mark 4:13

Parable is one of the key words of the Gospels. Jesus, like other Jewish teachers, taught by means of stories. In fact, although we usually do not think in such terms, Jesus is one of the greatest storytellers in the history of mankind. How many millions of people could tell you the story of the Prodigal Son or of Lazarus the Poor Man? With an economy of words that all writers must envy, Jesus presented his teaching by giving examples from life that have resonated in Western culture. Think of all that comes to mind, for instance, when we say the words "the lost sheep."

The advantages of telling stories to teach have to do with remembering and imagination. We remember stories because narrative sticks in our memory. They can teach us much because in a story there is an implied identification with what goes on. We are given access to an experience, for instance, of two men going to pray in the parable of the Pharisee and the publican. We can decide which of the men we can understand more, which is more sympathetic, who has more to teach us. If this were to be made explicit in propositions, it would be more awkward and less memorable. *It is possible to pray and to be pompous and proud. It is possible to think oneself righteous and misjudge others. It is possible to stand in a holy place and have thoughts that are really unholy. It is possible also that persons who are in situations that make them somehow alienated from religious experience are closer to God because of their spirit of repentance.* All of these conclusions are much easier to digest, to remember and to retell, when put as a parable: "Two men went up to the Temple to pray."

The parable referred to in this question is that of the sower and the seed. Even apart from its spiritual message, the parable is interesting in that the imaginative identification that it demands is not so much with the sower as with the seed. As in the Hans Christian Andersen story about the Christmas tree, we are asked to see plant life as a metaphor for human life. The parable is a tremendous example of the power of metaphor, because vegetable life is invested with symbolism and it is not at all difficult for us to accept.

Of course, that is perhaps because we have Jesus' own explanation of the parable. The disciples did not seem to catch the ball on the first bounce, but we are not in a position to judge them, because we have the answer key incorporated into the text. The commentary on his own parable is wonderfully spare writing. The sower sows the word (*logon* in the accusative form of the noun, which reminds us of the Jesus-Logos identification from the Gospel of St. John, "in the beginning was the Word"). Satan snatches the word from those who are on the wayside. The rocky ground represents those who have a shallow faith that does not persevere. The seed that grows among thorns is a metaphor for those for whom "the cares of this world" choke and kill faith. The seed in the good ground is symbolic of those who hear the word, accept it, and produce fruit.

The parable is a string of metaphors that provoke thought and invite to personal commentary. The human situation vis-à-vis the word of God is deftly sketched in a few lines. The examples are taken from an agricultural background but are easily understood and remembered by people from the city. The mystery of growth, the development that faith can take in our lives, the destiny implied in responding to the energy of the Word — all these are made accessible with a few words. Those who could never understand the abstractions of the previous sentence can understand this parable as a spiritual revelation.

Perhaps I should have written "*may* understand this parable," because there is always the possibility that we fail to understand. Thus Jesus' question here is for us: "Do you not understand this parable? How then will you understand the others?" This is not a kind of examination of reading comprehension. The understanding of the parable means getting closer to the spiritual reality it expresses. This is not just the question of what kind of ground you are, although, of course, that is part of the message. The other part is how you can make yourself the ground that is ideal for the word, one that results in the multiplication of growth symbolized by an abundant harvest.

First you must listen to the word. We may understand this in somewhat impersonal terms. The cacophony of modern life makes it hard to really listen to the word of God. There is so much background noise that it requires effort to concentrate in order to understand. However, this would not be exactly what Jesus is telling us. There is a power that opposes the word of God in this world, and that power is personal. Satan still tries to take away the seed of the word before it grows in us. While we should never be obsessed by the power of darkness, we should not be naïve and ignore our need to be zealous about our life of faith.

Those who do listen to the word must face the possibility of not persevering. Jesus presents two examples of such failure. The first is the seed that has shallow roots and cannot endure a time of dryness. Many people have a faith-life that is also shallow. Jesus referred to persecutions testing faith, but sometimes much less than a persecution can cause us to lose heart. Our identification with the cross of Jesus is so minimal at times that a small bit of suffering can shock us and test our faith. I suppose that some people think that faith is like an insurance policy that protects us from "the slings and arrows of outrageous fortune," but this is not belief in Jesus. Our faith does not remove the cross from our lives; rather it gives us the strength to bear it.

The second example of failure in discipleship is connected with luxury. Ralph Waldo Emerson, writing about the Dred Scott decision, said that it was such a shock because it revealed "that our prosperity had hurt us." Jesus is specifically warning us in the parable of the sower and the seed that comfort can be our enemy. Wealth can seduce us. By provoking desires, it can choke faith within us. As a missionary in a poor country I feel that this is a message especially important for North Americans.

The old phrase "the lap of luxury" applies to us as it has to no other civilization in the history of the world. We take so much for granted, even what would have seemed beyond the dreams of avarice to our grandparents. A lady once confessed to me that a chicken had wandered into her little yard and she had given it food and waited a few days to see if anyone came looking for it. Then she ate it, because she had not eaten meat in a long time. She was practically weeping because of her guilt, but I felt guiltier than she. In the United States, food is so abundant that we have to find ways to make it less nourishing, extracting natural fats, for instance. We have no idea of the scarcity in which people live in other parts of the world. And there are parts of the world — like sections of Africa that I have seen — that make El Salvador look prosperous.

The dangers of being choked by our desires are very real for us in our cornucopia culture of dangerous abundance. Our television reveals the excesses to which luxury propels us, and the Internet is a minefield of illicit desires. The question of Jesus — "Do you not understand this parable of the sower and the seed?" — should make us confront the reality of the danger to our faith all around us. We are more prone to worry about the contamination of our natural than of our moral environment. Both are important but the latter much more than the former. Spiritual life is even more important than physical life, after all.

How do we respond to the word of God? That is the interrogative behind this question of Jesus. If we understand the parable of the sower and the seed, we have a chance of understanding the other parables. That means that there exists for us the possibility of entering within the reality of God's mercy and his kingdom, the theme of so many parables.

Trying to wrestle with the meaning for me of this question of Jesus, I have used so many words, many more than the original parable. And I still don't know how to answer the question. I cannot say that I don't understand the parable, because I do see its message and feel challenged by it. If I say, "Yes, I understand it," however, then why don't I live completely dedicated to the word of God? Why do I feel put-upon sometimes? Why do so many other things distract me? Why can't I just multiply the blessing that has been given me? ◇

"Is a lamp brought in to be put under a bushel, or under a bed, and not on a stand?" — Mark 4:21

St. Thomas Aquinas was perhaps the most important Catholic theologian who ever lived. Among other projects he accomplished in his relatively short life (he died when he was only forty-nine years old) was a compilation of commentaries on the four Gospels. This was called the *Catena Aurea* — Latin for "golden chain" — and is a line-by-line commentary showing what Aquinas considered important insights of the Fathers of the Church and some of his predecessors in medieval theology on the Gospel verses.

The section of the *Catena Aurea* for this verse shows why it remains a treasure for Bible readers better than seven centuries after St. Thomas wove the interpretations together. St. Bede the Venerable had this to say about the image of the lampstand:

> The candle within us is that of our intellectual nature, and it shines either clearly or obscurely according to the proportions of our illumination. For if meditation, which feeds the light, and the recollection with which such a light is kindled, are neglected, it is presently extinguished.

The language of allegory, in which a particular thing stands for something else, is not so common now. However, we should get over the hurdle of style and think about our prayer life in terms of "feeding the light." Meditation is an essential element of the spiritual life. That is the greatest danger of our hurried pace of life. We do not have time to feed the light of faith. If you are always on your way to some other commitment, if you say that you do not have the "luxury" of time that is spent in peaceful reflection, then this message is for you.

I have learned the hard way how difficult it is to do ministry without meditation. A confessor of mine once said that we are like cisterns, and that, after serving up as much water as we have, we end up scraping sludge. We have to be constantly replenishing our spirit or we do harm to others and ourselves. Bede's observation is that meditation is the oxygen we need to keep the flame of faith alive. Without it, the light goes out and we end up in the dark. The next part of Bede's commentary is much less archaic in style:

> Or else the Lord warns His disciples to be as light, in their life and conversation, as if He said, "As a candle is put so as to give light, so all will look to your life. Therefore be diligent to lead a good life, set not in corners, but be you a candle."

I appreciate the directness of this: "Be you a candle." Years in the mission in El Salvador have given me real respect for candles. Although there was a time in the 1970s in the United States when scented candles seemed to be everywhere, in all sorts of colors, shapes, and sizes, I never appreciated candlelight until I lived through the war years in El Salvador. I arrived here in 1986, the exact middle of its civil war. Often the electric power would go out, sometimes for days at a time. I really was surprised to learn that candles actually did that trick of the movies of suddenly lighting up a whole scene. I had always thought that the directors had exaggerated, but many times since I came here I have done the same thing, removing the cover of darkness and "discovering" rooms.

Recently I went to baptize a newborn child whose parents thought that she was in danger of dying. It was after a Mass in Majaguey, one of the satellite chapels of Chirilagua, a community right alongside the Pacific. By the time Mass was over, it was near six, the hour that the sun sets and darkness invades the scenery. The house was "right here close by," which sometimes is a more than slight exaggeration. I decided that I would go immediately, somewhat to the surprise of the father of the child and the two prospective godparents, who went along for the ride and walk. The people lived in a poor shack of a house perhaps fifty meters from the beach.

There was no electricity, so when we entered the darkness of the small hut, the only light guiding us was from a crudely made oil lamp, a wick in a bit of a can. Near the bed on which lay the child, the father lit a candle so that I could read the prayers of baptism. I have prayed by candlelight many times, sometimes with older people who are sick; but for some reason the memory of the glow of the light of the candle and the small doll-like child in the middle of a cot covered with the woven straw *petate* sticks in my mind with unusual vividness. There we were, five of us adults crowded into the small alcove of the hut sharing the moment when the light of salvation dawned on the little girl.

The girl lived, I am so glad to say. Her father proudly showed her to me some weeks after the baptism. I hope that the light of faith also survives in both of them, for they have a hard life. That is where Bede comes in again. To keep the faith we must keep praying, "feeding the light." We have to find time and peace to do that.

And we have to be a light to others, "candles" that can illuminate the darkness that surrounds us. There is much that is wrong with this world and with us. That is what I mean by darkness. The power of sin exists in the world. It is behind the violence of this world, the selfishness that is everywhere, and, perhaps more importantly, in the confusion that does not always permit us to see what we are doing. Against the powers of darkness, Jesus, too, says, "Be you a candle." Or is light to be hidden? ◇

"With what can we compare the kingdom of God, or what parable shall we use for it?"   — Mark 4:30

Jesus' question here is rhetorical not in the sense of expecting a certain answer but because it announces a purpose. Jesus is about to give us a parable to study. The interrogative alerts us to take seriously what he is about to say. He asks in order to answer, as some professors do.

Teachers in the days of Jesus did not have lists of textbooks or articles to look up on the Internet. They taught by parables, which their students eagerly memorized. What we have in this passage from St. Mark is an introduction to class. The subject being studied is the kingdom of God. Jesus intends to give his listeners his doctrine about the involvement of God in human history.

The doctrine of the kingdom of God is one of the main themes of Jesus' preaching. The word for kingdom — in Greek, *basileia* — appears one hundred sixty-two times in the New Testament. Like most things important, it has been tremendously misunderstood. *Basileia* in Greek usage contains three separate meanings in most European languages. It means "kingdom" in the sense of an organized and even geographic state, but it can also mean "kingship" or "sovereignty," both with the idea of the person invested with authority (Christ's kingship) or of reign (Christ's rule over us).

Even in the time of Jesus' ministry in Galilee, people misunderstood his talk of the kingdom. In John 6:15, Jesus flees the people after the first multiplication of the loaves and fishes, "perceiving then that they were about to come and take him by force to make him king." It is interesting to think of the kingdom of Galilee that the people imagined. Did they think that from the green hillsides, which ringed the peaceful lake, armies would march out to conquer the world, like Alexander from Macedonia or the Romans from their city?

I think the best place to meditate on that idea would be from the hill on which stands the Church of the Beatitudes in Galilee. From the corridor outside the octagonal church you feel as though you could almost fly like an eagle over the small "sea" of Galilee. It gives you some feeling of the spiritual reign of Jesus. The imperial imagination is stimulated as you look across the deep blue water to the green necklace around it. The kingdom proclaimed in Galilee did conquer a good part of the world for a good long time, but it was not to be a kingdom of this world.

That was the hard part to understand, of course. Even after his death and subsequent Resurrection, Jesus was asked by his followers: "Lord, will you at this time restore the kingdom to Israel?" (Acts 1:6). Perhaps that indicates why we should not be surprised that his execution was based upon the charge brought against him that he wanted to make himself king instead of Caesar. That accusation prompted Pilate's question to Jesus, "Are you the king of the Jews?" (Matthew 27:11) and the dark irony of the *INRI* — the Latin initials for "Jesus of Nazareth, King of the Jews" — nailed to the head of the cross and still visible on our crucifixes.

It is a chastening thought to remember that Jesus died for the kingdom, even though those who put him to death had misinterpreted what he had meant by it. The lethal element makes this question of his more interesting and even dramatically ironic. He is seen in this passage taking pains to explain his kingdom, but we already know that his enemies would misunderstand it. Whatever parable or comparison he used, he would be mocked as he died as a would-be king. Is not one of the most poignant symbols of the Passion the crown of thorns?

For us the real question is what comparison or parable would *we* use to give an idea of the kingdom of God? If the kingdom of God seems to occupy the center of Jesus' preaching, shouldn't every Christian have some idea about what it is? If the kingdom was an "event" for Jesus, a "happening" in the history of the world, what does it mean for you and me?

Ulrich Luz has an interesting capsule definition of the kingdom for Jesus that could serve for any disciple. "The decisively new element in the preaching of Jesus about the kingdom of God," wrote the German Scripture scholar, "apart from Jesus' connecting the kingdom with his own mission, is the interpretation of *Basileia* as the universal and infinite love of God toward the unloved and marginated of Israel."

The kingdom of God is love. It is a very special kind of love, because it is both universal in application and infinite in depth. This differs from most of our experience of love, which tends to be concentrated in certain persons. Beyond that, our attractions are not usually to those most marginated. Even in the schoolyard, we see how certain people are more attractive than others because they are better looking, or because they have more abilities, physical or mental, or because they have more material things. What Jesus shows is the opposite of the superficial attractions that dominate our lives. The love of the kingdom is not about the categories of importance that we all learn in this world. It is something radically different.

What the kingdom represents in the teaching of Jesus has to be reflected in my life. There is not a day in which I do not pray, "Thy kingdom come." There are days, however, when I say the words and do not really invest myself in what I am saying. This is in spite of the fact that in El Salvador it is actually very hard to forget about the kingdom of God. There is so much poverty and injustice that it is difficult not to think about so much that is wrong with the world.

One recent morning the kingdom rang my doorbell in the person of a drunk looking for a handout (who was given the bum's rush by one of the deacons, unfortunately). It called again when the three women came to talk about their damaged houses. Then I visited one of the frontiers of the kingdom in the person of a friend whose cancer has returned. Later I met with the kingdom in a group of people who want to rebuild their chapel and their homes (in that order) after the destruction caused by two earthquakes in one month's time. Afterward I was aware of the kingdom in the two poor old people who want to be married in the Church before the husband dies. Then I met the kingdom in some children who did not sign up for communion classes because the fees were too expensive. I added another soul to the kingdom at Mass when I baptized a five-year-old girl. I recovered another confessing a young man who had lived in sin for six years. The kingdom, in its hope and promise, was present among the young people who were practicing for the live Stations of the Cross. My fatigue is the fatigue of the kingdom and likewise my contentment in having been able to do some good work this day. The kingdom is the mystery of the Church, which penetrates every moment of my existence, sometimes as a blessing, sometimes as a contradiction.

My consciousness of the kingdom today is the result of the fact that I was writing this small chapter before I started my pastoral odyssey. The kingdom stayed with me on my way through the day. Jesus' interrogative made me ask myself what comparisons I could make about the kingdom. It could do the same for you. ◇

"Why are you afraid? Have you no faith?" — Mark 4:40

In El Salvador, where I am working in the missions, in this year (2001) that I am writing this book, two very strong earthquakes shook the country and terrified most of its residents. In one way or another most of us here were asking ourselves about fear and faith, if not for ourselves, at least for others. There have been more than five thousand tremors after the two quakes, some of an intensity of five points on the famous Richter scale. Until you have lived through an experience of *terra firma* seeming to forget itself, it is not easy to imagine the panic that can surge through you when things start shaking and convulsing. The experience is a bit like the turbulence felt in some airplane flights, except that on the ground you have more of a right to expect a certain boring predictability and you can presume that everything wants to stay in its own place. Reading a book on St. Patrick, I encountered a phrase that I find interesting but not now self-evident for me: "The secret faithfulness of landscape." Here the landscape seems to be tired of the same-old, same-old — and evidently wants to be unfaithful.

It has been a kind of war of attrition on your nerves. Fear is so corrosive; with time it weakens what it cannot destroy altogether. As a pastor I cannot help but notice the fear of the people. Not even during the civil war here (twelve long years) did I see so many worried faces. I have felt called to preach confidence in God more than any other theme in these past few months. I think that pastoral leadership, like other kinds of leadership, requires a certain fearlessness. Fear is contagious, but so is courage.

Sometimes such things are easier to say than to live. One priest, quite upset by the tremors, was asked by an old woman if he ever was afraid. "You bet I am," he said. I appreciated his honesty, but I tend to think that simulated courage is better than no courage at all. A priest acquaintance was saying Mass when a tremor hit. Startled into panic, he started walking out of the church. Then he remembered where he was and what he had been doing and caught himself. He walked to the pulpit, which was a few steps from his path to the exit, and said to the parishioners who were making for the door, "Where do you think you're going? The tremor is over." They all returned to Mass. Recounting the incident to a group of his confreres, the priest smiled and said, "I think I fooled them."

A French writer once said that courage is the art of being afraid without appearing to be so. There is something of that in Christian faith. It is not that we are unaware of the dangers or that we don't feel the anxiety (we even mention the latter in the prayer after the Our Father at Mass). Rather it is that we have a confidence that supersedes our fears.

Jesus asks why the apostles are afraid. This question is not about the immediate cause of the apostles' panic. The Lord could feel the storm winds and see the water beginning to slosh into the boat. He looks beyond the present danger to the interior experience of desperation. That is why the question is twinned with, "Have you no faith?"

In the *Catena Aurea*, there is a reflection of St. Bede the Venerable about this passage that I find illuminating:

> And we also, when we were marked with the sign of the Lord's cross and determined to quit the world, we embarked in the ship with Christ. We attempt to cross the sea, but He goes to sleep, as we sail amidst the roaring of the waters, amidst the stirrings of our virtues, or the attacks of evil spirits of wicked men, or of our own

thoughts. And the flame of our love grows cold. Amongst storms of this sort, let us diligently strive to awake Him. He will soon restrain the tempest, pour down peace upon us, and give us the harbor of salvation.

Bede reflected about his own vocation as a monk, "when we were marked with the sign of the Lord's cross and determined to quit the world." However, what he says applies to every Christian following his or her vocation. We are all called to holiness, although not perhaps the monastic form of it. From baptism we were marked with the sign of the cross and so are not "of this world" as Jesus said. We sail sometimes amid the roaring of the waters, the stirrings of our souls, the attacks of evil spirits. The flame of our love grows cold, an image that is at the same time impossible and attractive.

The two key words in this twin question of Jesus are "cowardly" and "faith." Both of them merit our reflection. There is a difference between "afraid" and "cowardly" that the translation we are using does not reflect. "Cowardly" is not just being afraid but having fear in the face of trials or enemies. It is fear in relation to a situation. I think it would be better for us to understand the first part of this question as, "Why are you so cowardly?" It is both stronger language from the Lord and fits better with the accusation of not having sufficient faith. It also implies that Jesus is surprised at the lack of an interior attitude of self-discipline in his followers. Discipleship requires courage. The Christian asks himself or herself, "Could the Lord accuse me of cowardice?"

"Have you no faith?" is a question of supreme importance in the New Testament. The word used for faith, the Greek *pistis*, is one of the key words associated with Christianity. It appears as a noun some two hundred forty-three times in the books of the New Testament and in the form of a verb the same number of times. Its meaning includes both the idea of credibility (as in "Do you believe this is true?") and of personal confidence in the Lord ("Do you feel secure in me?"). Faith for the Christian includes both recognition of the Lord and his works and a personal relationship with him.

Thus the question posed by Jesus to the men in the boat with him has extraordinary resonance for us. He is asking us not only if we recognize his power but also if we have confidence in him. "Have you no faith?" is a question that has echoed down the centuries to all the followers of Jesus. It is a question directed to me and you. Do I believe in the power of the Lord to still the storms of my life? Do I have confidence in him despite the rocking of the boat and its shipping water?

There is a sad verse in the New Testament where the Lord asks, "Nevertheless, when the Son of man comes, will he find faith on earth?" (Luke 18:8). I remember that an unusually dramatic companion from my seminary studies had this verse scrawled on a piece of paper and taped to the wall in his room. It was practically the only ornament in the cell-like room. The obsessive character of the student matched one of the primary themes of Christianity. Do we have faith — in the deepest sense of the word?

I imagine myself in the boat on the newly calm sea, perhaps my heart still beating fast, hearing the Lord say, "Why are you so cowardly? Have you no faith?" ◇

"What is your name?" — Mark 5:9

This question comes from one of the strangest passages in the New Testament, in which Jesus exorcises the possessed man of the Gerasenes who lived among the tombs. The man has to be one of the most peculiar characters in the Bible, and his healing is both extraordinary and extraordinarily mysterious. We know hardly anything about him, besides his possession, and its bizarre consequence in the drowning of the herd of pigs.

He was a man with extraordinary physical strength, and no one was able to subdue him. Many times, says St. Mark, he had been bound, but he had succeeded in freeing himself, wrenching apart the chains and breaking the fetters. "Night and day among the tombs and on the mountains he was always crying out, and bruising himself with stones" (Mark 5:5).

When he sees Jesus, he runs to him and worships him. At the same time, he cries out, "What have you to do with me, Jesus, Son of the Most High God? I adjure you by God, do not torment me" (Mark 5:7). What is the meaning of this forlorn prayer? The man seems to ask the Lord in prayer not to have anything to do with him. He is so completely a prisoner of Satan that he sees contact with the Lord as "torment." Nevertheless he has bowed before Jesus and worshiped him. He believes that Jesus is the Son of God, and therefore knows what some of Jesus' own disciples ignore but is frightened by the knowledge.

What was the truth of this man's story? Could his possession be a metaphor for mental illness, just as in another part of the Gospel a fever is taken to be the consequence of an evil spirit? The human authors of the word of God had to describe revelation according to the categories of their understanding. If they understood that the fever that Peter's mother-in-law suffered was the work of an evil spirit, the curing of the fever had to be an exorcism. We can still see the redemptive power of Jesus restoring creation (which is the reason for most of the miracles) even if we don't see the necessity that the particular cure of the high temperature was an exorcism.

There is something spooky about mental illness, however. I know somebody who resembles the poor man of the Gerasenes. He is a relatively young man who lives in a rural parish in El Salvador. After the breakup of a bad relationship, he became mentally imbalanced. He refuses to wear clothes, and his mother keeps him chained to a small hut near the family home. This sounds incredible, perhaps — even incredibly cruel, but it is true. I went to his house, about an hour's difficult walk from the nearest road.

His mother thought the man possessed. She had tried various types of exorcisms (including attempts by several evangelical pastors) and cures, but they had all failed. When I first visited the man, he stared at me with the wonder of a small child. He repeated some of the phrases as I prayed for him, and almost all of the Our Father, which his mother thought a great change. However, he did not change much. Some nights he would spend screaming and some days he would be totally incoherent. He was not a bad-looking young man, and when I saw him, I thought of Ophelia's words about Hamlet, "O what a noble mind here is o'erthrown. . . . O woe is me to have seen what I have seen, see what I see." The sight of a human being so unhinged is so deeply disturbing.

When I asked about therapy, she could tell me a great deal about the inadequacy of mental health care in El Salvador. He had been hospitalized several times. Once he had come home almost normal but then refused the heavy medications that promised peace by sedation. I really don't know what could be done for the man. His family had tried countless schemes to have him take the medicine in food or drink, but he had always seemed able to detect it. The national psychiatric hospital, where he would have been injected by force, is worse than bedlam, where patients are left unattended. There is abuse of some patients by others, the mother told me. I know this sounds strange, but I ended up concluding that the mother did all that she could to take care of the man. At least living among his family, there was understanding and some peace.

I was less peaceful myself after several visits. He made the sign of the cross, generally, but sometimes would act afraid, and other times ignore me. Only the first time did the man seem to be very attentive. I did pray that God deliver him from whatever his problem was, mental illness or a demon. Many times since I met the man, I have thought of the Lord's miracle at Gerasa. Since at one point the medicine had worked partially, I am sure he has some kind of schizophrenia. The last time I saw his mother, she claimed he was better because he has become much calmer.

I suppose that a modern interpretation of the healing of the Gerasene demoniac would presume that he was also a victim of psychosis. There is a difficulty with reading the text in that way. The evangelist throughout his Gospel presents a mysterious aspect of the mission of Jesus, his antagonism with the demons who serve the "ruler of this world" (John 14:30, 16:11). The ministry of Jesus among men in St. Mark has a kind of metaphysical counterpoint of combat with evil spirits. Their abundance in the Gospel is seen particularly in this passage, where there is a "legion" of demons infesting one man. A Roman legion could include six thousand men.

What do we make of Jesus' rite of exorcism, which has this question as a part? In the Bible generally there was a power associated with knowing a name. When God gives Adam dominion over the other creatures, he tells him to name them. Naming the devil or an evil spirit involves overpowering it. We can see this in the folktale of Rumpelstiltskin, where knowledge of his name foils the evil power of the gnome. Jesus is claiming superiority over the demons by insisting on knowing, but we are lucky that it was decided to give only the corporate name. Otherwise we might have six thousand names fill the pages of the Gospel, rather like some people's forwarded e-mails.

Asking the name of the demon is not a question of curiosity; rather it somehow has to do with the battle between Jesus and the powers of darkness. That is a sense of the question that can provide us with something to meditate. What is the name of our demon (or demons)? What sorts of things separate us from God and men and have us howling among the tombs, metaphorically speaking? The older I get, the more aware I am of the multiplicity of my defects and distractions. Thomas Merton once said that demons dance over a monk's head near the time of matins. Sometimes they seem to be stomping about inside one's head.

It is said of Martin Luther that he was so conscious of the presence of the devil that he threw an ink-bottle at him once. What could be accomplished by said action is beyond my comprehension. (I can't imagine the devil worried about staining his wings.) There are Christians who can seem obsessed by the powers of darkness. It is an old heresy to think that the battle between good and evil has even sides and forget that Christ's victory is definitive. The power of the devil on earth is that of a retreating army. Without hope of victory, it tries to do as much damage as it can, like the Nazi troops retreating across Central and Eastern Europe.

On the other hand, we shouldn't minimize the supernatural. The great William Barclay, the Scottish Bible scholar whose commentaries were praised by Bishop Fulton Sheen, was sadly tinged by modernism. He read this story in his commentary on St. Mark as one of a simple cure. It probably occurred at night, he says, which explains the bizarre ambience of the miracle. The man *felt* as if a whole legion of demons was at work in him. He knew how the legions were, because he had seen them. Jesus had to sacrifice the swine because only if something really dramatic would happen could the man believe that he was healed. And we shouldn't feel bad for the pigs, says Barclay, because we all enjoy ham dinners.

The deliberate attempt to discount the supernatural reminds me of C. S. Lewis's complaint about scholars who strain at gnats but swallow the camel. We can believe that Jesus can dispose of the porcine multitude with a single gesture, but we don't want to talk about demons. We have to steer between the Scylla of obsessive attention to things satanic and the Charybdis of denying the supernatural struggle between the powers of good and evil that is invisible to us but nonetheless real.

"What is your name?" Jesus asks our demons. We should ask ourselves about our own demons, or perhaps about the weaknesses that the devil knows how to use in us. The story of the legion of devils can give us a new perspective on our own captivity to what opposes the Lord. The destruction of the herd of swine can be a great lesson for us.

It is a strange ending to a strange incident and would be especially vivid to a Jewish audience. Casting the demons into the swine is not necessarily funny, but there is something kosher and comic about all the possessed pigs jumping into the lake and dying. The pigs couldn't take the demonic possession this pericope seems to imply. The strangest note is that of the demons, spiritual beings that seem to need to dwell in some kind of flesh. If they can't have the man, they'll take the herd of pigs. Perhaps the best interpretation I have seen comes from the Navarre Bible. What happens to the swine is a sign of the destructive power of the demons. It is a warning of what demons could do to us. Better the pigs than us.

The question "What is your name?" was answered not by the man Jesus was healing but by his demon captors. I can't help thinking what might be the answer if the Lord asked me directly. While I haven't been howling among the tombs much lately, there are still contradictions in my life. Maybe what I need is for Jesus to confront me directly and in detail.

St. Bede the Venerable, in his commentary about this passage, talked about the need for confession in order to be set free from all that separates us from Christ. He comments on the strange experience of the man by pointing out:

> And even the priests of our time, who know how to cast out devils by the grace of exorcism, are wont to say that the sufferers cannot be cured at all, unless they in confession openly declare, as far as they are able to know, what they have suffered from the unclean spirits, in sight, in hearing, in taste, in touch, or any other sense of body or soul, whether awake or asleep.

The evangelist tells us that the Lord cast out seven devils from Mary Magdalene (cf. Mark 16:9). The man from the Gerasene country might have had as many as six thousand. How many you and I have would be an interesting — and perhaps terrifying — piece of information. ◇

And Jesus, perceiving in himself that power had gone forth from him, immediately turned about in the crowd, and said, "Who touched my garments?" — Mark 5:30

The woman had been sick for twelve years and had spent "all she had" in the process. Although she had seen "many physicians," she was actually worse than when she had begun. She suffered from a hemorrhage — the Greek is literally "the fountain of blood" — and this made her spiritually unclean according to Old Testament law. Her desperation had to make her desperate but not only that. She had to feel far away from God at the same time.

The Navarre Bible suggests that the spiritual uncleanness was the reason for her discretion in touching only Jesus' garment. She would have made Jesus unclean by touching him. Unlike the father of the young girl who could ask openly for a healing, this woman had to act surreptitiously.

St. Mark has some of her interior monologue about her motivation, in the literal translation of the Greek, "for she was saying if I may touch even the garments of him I will be healed" (Mark 5:28, *The New Greek-English Interlinear New Testament*). The woman has a great deal of faith in Jesus, a confidence that by only touching his garment she will end twelve long years of suffering.

It is an impersonal faith, however. This explains why Jesus asks this very puzzling question. Could he not have known who had touched him? Was his power like some kind of energy within that he could feel leaving him without his being involved intentionally? That would seem to pose a problem for the way we understand Jesus to be divine.

In the *Catena Aurea* this problem was met by a commentary by a writer mistakenly believed for a while to be St. John Chrysostom. Pseudo-Chrysostom, as he is called, wrote this about Jesus' question here: "But he asked, 'Who touched me?' that is, *in thought and faith,* for the crowds who throng around Me cannot be said to touch Me, for they do not come near to Me in thought and faith."

"Who are you?" Jesus was saying. He wants to change her impersonal faith in him to a personal relationship. Only she and Jesus know what happened. No one in the crowd, not even the disciples, has a clue about the secret drama of the situation. The disciples, quite typically in St. Mark, dare to criticize Jesus, serving as a kind of Greek chorus expressing the surprise the reader should feel about the question.

The woman has been caught. Even though she already feels that she is healed, she comes to Jesus in "fear and trembling." Twelve years of guilt pushed her down as she fell on her face before Jesus. The evangelist doesn't tell us, so we can only imagine the surprise of the crowd when the woman confesses to Jesus "the whole truth." Then Jesus says to her, "Daughter, your faith has made you well; go in peace, and be healed of your disease" (Mark 5:34).

In El Salvador, Jesus is sometimes familiarly called "Papa Chus." I was initially surprised at the title, which is familiar and tender. Didn't Jesus always talk about "the" Father? When did he call himself "Father"? Actually, in this miracle for the desperate woman, Jesus presents himself as a father figure. The woman becomes his "daughter," which is particularly striking because the Lord is on his way to curing another man's daughter. The impersonal relationship that the woman expected with Jesus, the healing she sought without ever speaking to him, was converted into the very personal and caring relationship expressed in Jesus' final words to her.

I would like to have known the woman's thoughts as she made her way home that night. She was finally well again in body, and spiritually she had received a tremendous blessing. "Daughter" he had called her. Her sickness had included with it an estrangement from God, but that had ended. She had touched God and she was now healed.

The incident in which this question occurs — as well as the question itself — makes me think of how close God is to us. Aristotle once said that it was ridiculous to think that Zeus would interest himself in men's daily affairs. Zeus was for the philosopher the Prime Mover, transcendent to the point of being far away from human concerns. There are people for whom it is that way. God is completely other, to the point of being separated from all our life. Our God is a touchable God.

The First Epistle of St. John bears witness to that mysterious truth: "That which was from the beginning, which we have heard, which we have seen with our eyes, which we have looked upon and touched with our hands, concerning the word of life — the life was made manifest, and we saw it, and testify to it, and proclaim to you the eternal life" (1 John 1:1-2).

St. Luke emphasized the touchable God in the account of Jesus' Resurrection appearance to the eleven apostles. When they are frightened at seeing him, he says, "Handle me, and see; for a spirit has not flesh and bones as you see that I have" (Luke 24:39). In Jesus we have a God so close to us that we can touch him. There is a Spanish hymn that speaks of this that we sing in La Libertad: "So close to me that I can touch him."

God is close to us, but sometimes we are not close to him. Often it is only by paradox that we can express the truth about God. He is closer to us than we are to ourselves, and yet we can be interiorly so far away from him. The story of this desperate woman reminds us that we can be in need of God and want his healing but not want to deal with him personally.

The idea of God as an impersonal power seems to be something alien to us. But is it really? There are novena chain letters still found in our church pews, and people sometimes pray for intentions without really praying to God. We want God's power, but we don't dare sometimes (or don't care at other times) to meet him face to face. We can be like the poor woman to whom Jesus addressed this question.

Have I touched Jesus' garment but not talked to him? Have I wanted something from him desperately but not bothered to deal with him personally? Is what I really need to do is to fall down before him and tell him "the whole truth"? The answer to all these questions is "yes." Don't I need for Jesus to lift me up and tell me that I am his child?

In other words, don't I need to experience Jesus like this woman did? Again the answer to both of these is "yes."

What about for you? ◇

"Why do you make a tumult and weep? The child is not dead but sleeping."   — Mark 5:39

O n the way to Jairus's house, Jesus healed the woman with the hemorrhage. While he was still speaking to the woman, people came from Jairus's house to say that it was too late to do anything for the little girl. Why bother the teacher now? Jesus immediately told the distressed father, "Do not fear, only believe" (Mark 5:36). His attention to the man's needs is striking although typical.

Arriving at the house, there is "a tumult" and people are wailing and weeping. Mourning was expected to be a noisy activity in the culture of Jesus. It was also something essentially public. This is so in many places and cultures in the world even today. Where I live and work, it would not surprise me to go to a home where a child has died and encounter near chaotic conditions. Schedules are more flexible in agricultural societies, and people are not shut out of events by work schedules or by the structure of urban housing. That means that one's emotional life is often in the public domain and stiff upper lips are not *de rigueur*.

In the chaos of emotion in Jairus's house, Jesus is clearly the eye of the storm. He asks this question of the loud mourners and it does not matter to him that they respond by laughing at him. He proceeds to chase everyone out of the house except his favorite trio of apostles — Peter, James, and John — and the parents of the twelve-year-old girl who was supposedly dead. Going in to where the girl lay, he takes her hand and says, "Little girl, to you I say, arise" (Mark 5:41, *The New Greek-*

English Interlinear New Testament). And the girl "immediately" gets up and walks around.

There are further problems with this passage, such as Jesus' saying that he doesn't want anyone to know of the miracle, but they do not concern us here. What is interesting to us is the question to the mourners. Had the girl really only been sleeping? This is hardly likely. The miracle obviously shows Jesus' power to raise the dead, which thus relativizes death to the point that we can compare it to sleep.

St. Bede in the *Catena Aurea* says as much: "For to men she was dead, who were unable to raise her up; but to God she was asleep, in whose purpose both the soul was living, and the flesh was resting, to raise again. Whence it became a custom among Christians that the dead, who, they doubt not, will rise again, should be said to sleep."

The Roman poet Virgil said that Sleep was "Death's brother," but perhaps St. Bede had it correctly, that this Gospel passage was the source of the practice that some Christians have of using sleep as a metaphor for death. I remember that the pastor of the parish in which I grew up almost always pointed out at funerals that our word "cemetery" came from the Greek word for "sleeping chamber." Some Christian religious groups in the Reform tradition, who do not believe that the soul goes immediately to God, also talk about people sleeping in their graves until judgment day. This is reflected in Edgar Lee Masters's wonderful *Spoon River Anthology*, which is a cycle of poems about the dead in the Spoon River cemetery, in which the introductory verses have as a refrain, "All, all, are sleeping on the hill."

Interpreted in the light of the Resurrection miracle, the question can be taken as a criticism of excessive grief. Why do we weep and wail at the death of a loved one? Do we doubt the power of Jesus to raise the dead? Our response to the news of death should always be to listen to Jesus' words: "Do not be afraid, only believe" (Mark 5:36, *The New Greek-English Interlinear New Testament*).

I have had the need of listening to these words of Jesus two times, especially in the last few months. Both times the death of a young friend took me by surprise in the worst sense of those familiar words. Although I was very concerned about consoling both families, and I made sure that all knew that it was okay to mourn and to cry, because even Jesus wept at the tomb of his friend Lazarus, I felt a bit empty inside. I myself could not cry, for instance, although I came close.

It would have been better to cry, I think. What I did instead was retreat a bit from God into a kind of stunned silence. I was resentful. Why did such young persons have to die? Both friends had been very spiritual young men. I had been both their confessor and their friend. The two of them had had some presentiments of their early deaths, and I had discounted their premonitions not because I disbelieved their intuitions but because I did not want to accept them. There had been preparation, I realized, but that did not console me at all.

One of the young men had died on his way to the States on the perilous route of illegal entry. He had died in an accident and I had heard that the body had been disfigured. I remember thinking, "Maybe it is not him; maybe there is some terrible mistake." Fortunately, I only admitted such wishful thinking to one other person. Still, it stung me. In the case of the other death, I was told at the wake that the man had asked to see me before he died. I had been called only a few hours before his death in the middle of the night, and he was hours away because I had been transferred to another parish. Disappointment made for frustration and that translated into the sense of powerlessness that breeds resentment.

I am afraid that I would have laughed at Jesus with the mourners. Grief sometimes needs a scapegoat, a target for anger. In the case of Lazarus, the brother of Martha and Mary, I hear resentment even in the words of Martha when she says to Jesus, "Lord, if you had been here, my brother would not have died" (John 11:21). One of the brothers of the man who died in the accident wanted to blame the *coyote*, as the person who leads illegal immigrants across the borders is called. I heard another sibling tell him in a long-distance telephone conversation, "I know you think we are too complacent, but we can never have our brother back anyway. We have to give him to God." Of course, the second brother was right, I thought, but my sympathy was with the one who could not accept the death.

Remembering this sadness still stirs my emotions. I know, however, that I have to listen to the voice of Jesus saying, "Why do you make a tumult and weep? The child is not dead but sleeping" (Mark 5:39).

We are objective except in our own cases. We can console others but many times not ourselves. What all of us need is to listen to the Lord. I have taken this question much to heart because of the freshness of my grief. I have hardly had time to think about how you might read this. Maybe you feel the same way I do, or maybe you know someone like me. Either way, this question can help you reflect on the power of Jesus in our lives. He who calmed the sea can give peace to our hearts also. "Why all this desperation?" he says to us. "I am here to take things in hand." ◇

And he said to them, "How many loaves have you? Go and see."   — Mark 6:38

Jesus is showing his Irish side again, responding to a question with a question. To paraphrase Mark 6:37, the disciples have asked, rather sarcastically, "Shall we go and spend a fortune — two hundred days' wages — to buy them all some bread?" Jesus asks somewhat prosaically, "And how many loaves do you have?" Undoubtedly, this disconcerted the disciples. There is nothing worse for conversation than having your sarcasm completely ignored. Jesus charges on beyond them and puts them to counting the loaves they have. I am not surprised that he adds "go and see" to the question — understood as in "right now." I imagine that the disciples were looking at Jesus as teenagers sometimes gaze at their benighted and ignorant parents who have just requested something they consider impossible.

The reluctance of the disciples is, of course, understandable. This is the first miracle of the multiplication of food. They were overwhelmed with the logistics of the situation. There were thousands of people gathered to hear the Master, in a desolate place, and the hour was late. I am sure that the disciples thought they were being very clever anticipating the problem of food and suggesting that Jesus send them all home. Their concern was quite logical and their solution reasonable, although there is a suggestion in the Gospel narrative that perhaps the disciples wanted to be rid of the crowd. Perhaps their practicality had to do with their concern about managing Jesus.

The Master's command to the crowd to arrange itself in groups of hundreds and fifties must have made the Logistics

Group a bit nervous. With only five loaves and two fishes, what can he possibly hope to accomplish? Perhaps some of those closest to Jesus were the ones who were most surprised by the miraculous feeding of the five thousand. The mysterious rite of blessing and breaking and the laborious process of sharing the food must have fascinated them, but I think that the disciples were probably more astonished than anyone by the twelve baskets of fragments left over.

There is a modernist interpretation of the miracle that perverts the whole sense of Jesus' ministry to the crowd by this miracle of the loaves and fishes. According to this supposedly practical reading, the people had some food hidden among them and Jesus' gesture helped all of the selfish to let loose with what they had and reveal that there had always been more than enough for everyone. That would be a great trick but would not be a miracle showing the divine power of Jesus. It would also involve a kind of hoax, because the disciples could not honestly distribute food offered by others as if it had been blessed by their Master.

I think that this miracle speaks especially to the ministry of the Church. The contrast between the disciples' concern and the Lord's compassion should get our attention. The disciples had expressed concern for the people. They had presumed that there was no way for them to feed all those listening to Jesus. And they had been wrong. The first lesson of the miracle was for the disciples. Of course, they didn't quite get it — we will see that later — but the miracle is primarily about ministry nonetheless.

I apply this question about the loaves and fishes to my ministry. I am a pastor of a town of fifty thousand people with a ninety-percent Catholic population. We are two priests to shepherd the large flock of very poor people. This is the second time that I am pastor here, and during the years I was gone, life for them has become more difficult. I was sent to the parish right after one earthquake and before another. Although there were few deaths related to the catastrophes in this town, the earthquake has badly damaged the local economy. The people are poorer than ever and, among the young, desperation reigns. For many, the only thing hopeful is to dream of going to the United States.

A sense of hopelessness is sometimes waiting for us at the corner and shadowing us all the day long in La Libertad. I look at the people filling the market outside the rectory or waiting in lines for buses and I think about Jesus' remark about the sheep without a shepherd. Like the disciples, I would like the Lord to send the people to where they can be fed and taken care of. And then I feel that he is telling me, "You give them something to eat" (Mark 5:37).

Obviously this is not to be taken just in the literal sense of feeding people, although sometimes there is a question of real hunger. There are, in fact, so many material needs. Every day, people are at my door in the mission asking for help with something. One of the many town drunks recently asked me to pay for medicine to clean up some cuts he got in a fight with some erstwhile friends. I could send him to the parish clinic, but there are cases that need more help, like questions of surgery. Again, like the disciples, I say, "Where is the money going to come from?" I have financial worries for the first time in my life, because the mission is cutting budgets. I am not quite counting the tortillas yet, but I am much more sensitive to the money going out than what is coming in. The needs always seem greater than the means. I can appreciate the point of view of the apostles.

People need God more than material things, however. There is poverty in El Salvador but not like what I saw in Africa, for instance. I do not think that the Church routinely has to set about feeding people. They should be able to feed themselves. But at a certain level, the interest of the Church in human dignity demands some application to the problem of poverty.

This is not something the Church does alone but which she cannot forget either. Jesus makes that clear in the passage we are thinking about here: that the material welfare of our fellow human beings is always important for us.

More than meals, however, the Church must attend to the souls of the poor. She must give them hope and signal God's loving care for them. This question reminds me that the Lord asks me to get the people organized in groups and to share the mystical meal that is our religion. "How many loaves have you?" he says to me; "What do you have to start with?" in other words, to help these people. What little there is of bread or fish has to be blessed, broken, and shared.

"How many loaves have you?" Jesus says to the ministers of each community in the Church. It means that we have to hustle up the few loaves and fishes available and put them into Jesus' hands. That is how I understand this question and meditate upon it as a minister of the Church.

"How many loaves have you?" Jesus says to every Christian. The ministry has to do some of the detail work, but there must be an offering to start with. In the multiplication miracle as it is reported in chapter 6 of St. John, we have a detail that the other Gospels do not tell us. A young boy is the one who has the loaves and fishes. We don't know his name, but we all have heard of him. He played an important part in the miracle by offering his loaves and fishes.

The boy had been carrying a poor man's supper. Barley loaves cost less than bread made with wheat. Although he could have been selling the food — as children are so often sent to sell food among the poor (something I see every day) — I think he may have been carrying the meal to his father. St. Mark emphasizes the men who were listening to Jesus. St. Matthew mentions that there were women and children also, but it would certainly be more cultural for the men to listen to the one whom people were saying was the Savior of Israel.

In a society in which fast food did not exist, it would not be unlikely that a woman would send a son to give her husband food. A Mexican immigrant working in the United States once told me that his first job was being a "lunchero," which he defined as carrying his father's lunch to where he was working in the fields. It was an important job, because it helped his father to work longer and produce more.

Whatever the motivation for the boy being in the crowd with his humble food, he can stand as a figure for all of us. Maybe you are the one with the five loaves and two fishes. Then this question of Jesus means you will have to offer what you have so that Jesus can feed his people. Did the boy overhear Jesus saying to his disciples, "How many loaves have you?" Did he volunteer what he had?

Whether you hear this question, or overhear it, you can profit by it. Is Jesus saying to you, "Look at all the problems of the world, how much people need. What can you do about it?" Do you say, "Here is what I have; please use it"? ◇

"Then are you also without understanding? Do you not see that whatever goes into a man from outside cannot defile him, since it enters, not his heart but his stomach, and so passes on?"   — Mark 7:18-19

One of the most important things Jesus taught was about the importance of the interior life. The Gospels record that the greatest conflict Jesus had was not with the Roman oppressors of his people, nor with the guerrilla forces contrary to them, but with the Pharisees. These were religious people, but their religion was based on externals. Their concern was always to fulfill the letter of the Law of Moses but without regard to the inner motivation.

A religion of externals requires a great deal of fastidiousness — about diet, about hygiene, about the business of life — but not always a great deal of love. To give just one example of Jesus' teaching in contrast to a religion of externals, we can look to the parable of the Good Samaritan. A Jewish woman convert once gave me a reading of the parable in terms of Jesus' polemic about true religion that I cannot forget. We were sitting on a balcony at the Notre Dame Center in Jerusalem, just opposite the gates of the Old City. She told me that the parable of the Good Samaritan was a key for her understanding of Christianity.

Her interpretation of the parable had to do with the definition of what was unclean in the Law of Moses. According to the religion of the Pharisees, a person who touched a corpse was unclean. That may explain why the priest and Levite pass by the victim whom the Samaritan helps. My teacher, a formidable woman who worked as a lawyer on behalf of Palestinians, thought that both men might have been concerned about ritual purity. Because they were probably on their way to the Temple, they couldn't stop and see a man who was perhaps dying. It would complicate their day, and perhaps make them unclean for their religious duties. Their religion actually got in the way of their charity.

Jesus preached that uncleanness was not based on external things, what you touched or ate or happened to you, but was something that started in the heart. He had been explaining this to the crowd of people just before this bit of dialog with his disciples. These did not understand what he was saying, because it was contrary to the religion they had learned from childhood. As Jews they felt that it did matter what kind of food you ate, how it was prepared and served, how you dressed, what brushed up against you, etc. In private with the Lord, the disciples take up the issue. What did he mean?

The text says only that they "asked him about the parable." There might have been more to it than that. When Jesus asks them, "Then are you also without understanding?" we can take this as a reproach. In Romans 1:31, lack of understanding is listed with the vices of those who resist God. It might have been that the disciples, asking Jesus about the implications of his teaching, were actually resisting what he had said. Some people ask for "explanations," but they really want retractions. It would be consistent with St. Mark to show that resistance, and Jesus' words are meant to be critical.

"Of all people, I thought you would understand" is a common reproach among friends and former friends. That is more or less the sense of this question of Jesus. He is saying that he expects his disciples to understand his preaching about interior motivation and religion more than anyone else would.

That is how we can take this question for our own meditation. Jesus is asking us, "Do you understand what really matters in a person is what comes from the heart?" This is something we should apply to other people, but that should be applied first and foremost to ourselves.

There are several key words in the question that merit our attention. First of all, we need to see the failure to understand as a resistance to understanding. Jesus is saying, "Do you still resist this teaching?" Sometimes our not understanding is culpable. It is really not a misunderstanding at all; it is willful rebellion and resistance to insight.

If we take this question as though it were addressed to us, we have to think about whether we have resisted believing in the message of interior religion that Jesus taught. Another key word in the implied dialog is translated here as "defile." What defiles a person? Jesus taught that it was sin that defiled, not accidents of food or drink, or anything external to a man or extrinsic to his intentions. While we don't talk much about "defilement" nowadays, we do judge people sometimes by criteria that are extrinsic to the heart.

Obviously, the Bible asks us not to judge people at all, leaving that to the Almighty Judge. However, we tend to classify people by external categories. We feel sympathy for them on the basis of what really comes from outside of them, if they are clean, or poor, or have the same culture as we do, or if they dress differently, or don't have the same norms of etiquette.

So much of what we feel about others has to do with considerations of class or chance. It is easier for us to sit down at a table with a person of our own type of background — or from one more prosperous than ours — although that person could be an adulterer, or someone who has committed fraud, than to sit down with a homeless person, who perhaps smells bad but has not been guilty of anything but having bad luck.

"Defilement," which means the ruin of a person by rebellion from God, is not based on externals. What matters is what comes from the heart. Jesus went on to teach his disciples on the kinds of things that can defile: "evil thoughts, fornication, theft, murder, adultery, coveting, wickedness, deceit, licentiousness, envy, slander, pride, foolishness" (Mark 7:21-22).

The vices in the above list ought to scare us and they actually flow out of our hearts (another key word). Jesus in this teaching is like the character "The Shadow" in the old radio plays. "Who knows what darkness lurks in the hearts of men?" asked the introduction to each segment, followed by, "The Shadow knows." For the Christian, it is a fact of our experience that Jesus knows not only "the heart-ache and the thousand natural shocks / that flesh is heir to," as Shakespeare's Hamlet phrases it (III.i.56) but also how rebellion takes over the seat of our intentions, the heart.

Do we resist this teaching? Do we try to reduce religion to something that will not invade the heart? Is our religion based upon appearances, or on circumstances that are really outside of the personal intentions? Do we underestimate the rebellion that nests in our hearts? How far are we from the purity of heart that Jesus taught was the most important thing in our relationship with God?

John Donne has a beautiful sonnet on the subject of the heart and its resistance to God. It is worth our thoughtful reflection:

> Batter my heart, three person'd God; for you
> As yet but knock; breathe, shine, and seek to mend;
> That I may rise, and stand, o'erthrow me, and bend
> Your force, to break, blow, burn, and make me new.
> I, like an usurp'd town, to another due,
> Labour to admit you, but O, to no end.
> Reason, your viceroy in me, me should defend,
> But is captived, and proves weak and untrue.
> Yet dearly I love you, and would be loved fain,
> But I am betroth'd unto your enemy;
> Divorce me, untie, or break that knot again,

Take me to you, imprison me, for I,
Except you enthrall me, never shall be free,
Nor ever chaste, except you ravish me.

— *Holy Sonnets*, XIV

We need to pray that Christ will conquer our hearts, which are like the "usurp'd [that is, captured] town" in Donne's imagery. We need him to lay siege to us, to liberate us from "Satan and all his pomps." The heart has to be taken by Christ. Jesus taught that the heart was the source of so many bad desires and evil actions. If we understand and do not resist his teaching we have to pray like the poet that the Lord himself vanquish our complicity with what defiles us and set us free almost in spite of ourselves.

Surrender yourself to the Lord. That would be truly understanding. ◇

"How many loaves have you?"   — Mark 8:5

The famous baseball player and world-class malaprop Yogi Berra purportedly said about the recurrence of something, "Déjà vu, all over again!" The redundancy is what makes for a comic note here, although, in general, repetition in speech tends to bore us, sometimes to desperation. How many times have people tested our patience using without shame phrases like "At the risk of repeating myself"? Here in El Salvador the catch phrase for repeaters is "May the repetition be useful." Of course it seldom is, in terms of the argument, but there is another popular saying that is applicable here: "Repetition is the mother of learning."

No doubt the repetitions in the Bible are related to the brute necessity we have of learning by repetition. But life repeats itself as well. In the case of the context of this question of Jesus, the disciples seem to have forgotten the first miracle of the multiplication of the loaves. Once again, Jesus is teaching a multitude in a desert place. He tells his disciples to feed the people. "How can we give so many men bread in the desert?" they ask. It is as if we were back to square one. They regress to their feeling of impotence before the situation, just as they did the time before.

Jesus asks almost ritually — automatically, ignoring the tone of the disciples — "How many loaves have you?" That should have recalled the first miracle, and perhaps it did. They respond, "Seven." This is an important point because the difference in number distinguishes the second from the first miracle, along with a few other details. There were five loaves in the first miracle, and two fishes. This time there are "a few small fish" (Mark 8:7), and the emphasis seems to be clearly on the bread. There are seven baskets left over afterward, while there were twelve the last time.

As I write this reflection, the bells of the church are sounding, calling people to the first Mass of Sunday. It is a quarter of an hour before seven on a morning that is already very warm. Heat is an existential category in the tropics but especially at this time of year, when the rains are about to start. There is something almost metaphysical about the humidity at this moment. I have a long day ahead of me. Before six hours pass I will celebrate three Masses, hear an hour of confessions, and attend people in the office for another hour. The number of people I will see and their diverse needs is somewhat daunting for me.

I feel like the disciples in the situation that prompts Jesus' question here: What will I give all these people? Jesus' question for me is, "What do you bring to this?" He will do the miracle of taking care of the people but asks what I can contribute. He is the one breaking the bread at the Eucharist, although he uses my hands. He is the one giving bread to the hungry heart of his people — I only have to remind them of that.

The other little chapter about this question — "How many loaves have you?" — led me to think about the real physical hunger in this world, which is more than a metaphor for all the injustices and problems that exist this side of paradise. However, this time the question provokes in me thoughts of the Eucharist. What do we bring to the Masses I will celebrate this morning? This is not only about the bread and wine we will share. It is also about how all of us together this morning, in each congregation and individually, bring something for the Lord to break and bless.

Just as in the case of the disciples from this part of St. Mark, we don't have much to bring. But what we have we must put in the hands of Jesus. He has to break it and bless it. There is something important to meditate on in the implied violence of the Eucharist. The bread is broken, as something in us has to break also. Maybe that is what the enigmatic Scripture means about the violent bearing away the kingdom of God (cf. Matthew 11:12).

The English poet Percy Bysshe Shelley's *Prometheus Unbound* has a phrase that has stayed with me down the years, "hecatombs of broken hearts." Shelley was alienated from God when he wrote the poem, and so wrote of his defiance of a god (Zeus, from the Greek pantheon) who demanded the sacrifice of so many hearts. A hecatomb was the ritual in which a hundred bulls were slaughtered and offered to the divinity. The poet has Prometheus accuse the god of requiting man's worship "with fear and self-contempt and barren hope."

Of course that accusation is completely wrong when one thinks of Jesus the God who sacrifices himself, the God who suffers. Shelley, unfortunately, didn't get as far as Jesus in the Bible, I am afraid. But the resentment of "hecatombs of broken hearts" doesn't just exist among people explicitly angry with God like Shelley. We believers sometimes think that our faith asks too much of our hearts. This is matched by a symmetric error of minimizing what is expected of us and not take seriously the breakage that has to happen when we fall into the hands of Jesus. Both the resentment and the reductionism are very wrong.

Why did Jesus have to break the bread? Couldn't he have multiplied the loaves without tearing them? Obviously this is a small detail, but one I find meaningful. The Eucharist is the breaking and blessing of bread. Apparently the bread had to be broken to be blessed. I think that it is ditto for us. In some way blessedness follows brokenness. We are all accustomed to the phrase "to die to self." The paradoxical promise of Christianity is that by denying ourselves we will be fulfilled. Unfortunately, this is so much rhetoric until what we call moments of truth arrive.

Perhaps in the vast crowd that was listening to Jesus that day, there were some who actually had some bread stashed away. Maybe they thought it would be imprudent to mention that they had some stores in their possession. They *knew* that there was no way that their bread could feed the multitude, so why bring up the fact that they still had something? Their own bread must have tasted funny when the blessed bread was passed around.

So will ours if we don't give it all to Jesus.

"How many loaves have you?" ◇

And he sighed deeply in his spirit, and said, "Why does this generation seek a sign? Truly, I say to you, no sign shall be given to this generation." — Mark 8:12

I am reading a work that is purportedly a scholarly study of St. Paul. The author remarks as if it were simply a matter of fact that St. Paul thought that his generation was the last to live on the earth. In this, says the author, he resembled "the man Paul called his Lord" because Jesus thought that his was the last generation also. This is not by any means a new theory but one that has been around since the late nineteenth century. None other than the famous humanitarian Albert Schweitzer held the same theory about Jesus.

These "scholars" get these kinds of theories from hints in the Scripture texts. In St. Mark, Jesus criticizes his generation quite strongly. They had rejected the Son of God, the Savior. They hid their lack of faith behind a desire to see miracles and yet despite all of Jesus' miracles they did not believe. Their failure to recognize the Messiah was the worst calamity that could have happened to a human generation.

There is a certain fierceness about Jesus' commentaries concerning this subject, something that can surprise and alarm us. His contemporaries were a generation "adulterous and sinful," Jesus says a little bit beyond this passage (cf. Mark 8:38). In Mark 13:30, he says that the present "generation will not pass away before all these things take place." From its context, the remark means such things as the sun being darkened, the moon eclipsed, the stars falling from the sky, and the "powers of heaven" shaken. The implication is that it was almost the end of the game. The clock was running out.

The supposed scholars are surprisingly literal about reading these words of Jesus. The error must have been his, they think. They absolve both the ones who wrote down what he had said and those who interpret them in the most limited sense possible. Nevertheless, it is possible to give a symbolic interpretation to his words. Wasn't something happening to the people that went much beyond the prophetic and apocalyptic imagery of the sun and the moon and stars? How would you describe, in the vocabulary of prophecy current at the time, the opportunity to be in communion with the Savior of the human race? What could be said of the chance to meet the invisible and omnipotent God in a contemporary?

In this, as in all Bible passages, it is very important to look at the meaning of the specific words used. The word "sign" here means something very definite. The Jewish people were waiting for centuries for some final manifestation of God's plan for the human race. In this plan for the entire world, they were, according to the prophets, destined to play the most important role. Neither of their kingdoms (the people of Israel had been divided into two kingdoms for a long time) had been as impressive as the empires that rose and fell around them. Nevertheless, the idea of empire had been assimilated into the soul of the prophetic tradition. Israel would be a spiritual empire, her prophets concluded against all reason and historical logic. All nations would come to Jerusalem to worship God, said the prophet Isaiah and others.

The Babylonians replaced the Assyrians and were subjugated eventually by the Persians. Alexander the Great subjected the territories included in the three empires and extended his reign even further. The Hellenic empires that came to be after the death of Alexander were eventually conquered by the Romans, who then fought between themselves until establishing what was the greatest empire ever seen around the Mediterranean basin. And meanwhile the people of Israel were conquered, managed brief moments of subject-state autonomy, changed forms of government, and changed masters. This was a process of centuries. But when would what the prophets prophesied materialize?

The spiritual leaders held that there would be signs. Jesus himself several times referred to the signs that the people needed to heed. When the disciples of John the Baptist come to him to ask whether or not he is the Messiah, he says, "Go and tell John what you have seen and heard: the blind receive their sight, the lame walk, lepers are cleansed, and the deaf hear, the dead are raised up, the poor have good news preached to them" (Luke 7:22).

The messianic signs would confirm the realization of God's plan. The new world order would be spiritual and mean the end of injustice and the perfect peace. The corruption of the world would give way to God's justice. There were many things mixed in here, but we still believe in the basic content of the vision. Israel played the key role in the development of a new order, the kingdom of God. The empire longed for by the prophets would actually be the empire of Jesus.

The word itself ultimately derives from two Latin words that mean "to set in order." Jesus inaugurated a new empire of the spirit, with dimensions far beyond the dreams of an oppressed people who had been on the margin of power for centuries. However, when he announced this empire of the spirit, it was not recognized as such. There is a mysterious irony about the proclamation of the kingdom of God in the midst of so many other dreams of empire. The people were looking for another kind of sign than that offered by Jesus.

In St. Matthew's Gospel, a number of scribes and Pharisees say to Jesus, "Teacher, we wish to see a sign from you" (Matthew 12:38). Jesus says that the only sign to be given will be "the sign of the prophet Jonah" (Matthew 12:39). St. Mark does not mention the sign of Jonah (that is found in St. Matthew), a reference to the mystery of the Resurrection. Here Jesus says only that the generation will not receive a sign. Can we not conclude that he means the kind of sign that the people were expecting? St. John tells us that at one point, Jesus had to flee the people because they wanted to make him their king. There was, of course, the deadly irony of the Gospel at work here. Jesus was, of course, their king but not the kind of king they wanted. This mistake about the king was the most dramatic and catastrophic misunderstanding in history.

It is not a misunderstanding limited to one generation, however. Jesus' words about his generation and about the signs of the fulfillment of God's plan could easily apply to our own time. There is an eternal now about the Gospel and about the message of Jesus. It is always *this* generation that is seeking a sign, the generation alive today. In that eternal now, our own generation should feel itself alluded to in Jesus' preaching about the definitive character of the present time. At the turn of the millennium, many people took seriously the notion of the end of the world like never before. Couldn't we say that many are still looking for a sign? Isn't their faith on hold until they are entirely convinced?

The question here is thus for us, and so is the sigh of frustration. "He sighed deeply in his spirit." A sigh from a friend or loved one is sometimes a thousand times worse than a shout. How hard it is to disappoint someone we care about. What if we disappoint Jesus? More than the question, the sigh haunts me. What about you? ◇

And being aware of it, Jesus said to them, "Why do you discuss the fact that you have no bread? Do you not yet perceive or understand? Are your hearts hardened? Having eyes do you not see, and having ears do you not hear? And do you not remember? When I broke the five loaves for the five thousand, how many baskets full of broken pieces did you take up?" They said to him, "Twelve." "And the seven for the four thousand, how many baskets full of broken pieces did you take up?" And they said to him, "Seven." And he said to them, "Do you not yet understand?"   — Mark 8:17-21

Here we have a whole series of questions, but all of them are summarized in the last, "Do you not yet understand?"

I have a school in my mission parish of which I am the nominal director. There are Salvadoran Franciscan Sisters involved in the administration and teachers appointed by the government as well. Although I do not give the work the attention that I would like to, I teach the ninth graders one hour of instruction in the faith per week. One morning I had a session with the young people that left me a bit disappointed. About half the class puts no effort into studies. I gave them my own version of "Do you not yet understand?"

The experience of teaching is not the only one in which we can feel the frustration that Christ seems to have felt here. There are friends to whom one would like to make a list of misunderstandings. Parents, of course, have a similar — although more painful — experience. I read a letter the other day from a woman who said that she agreed with another who had said that although she loved them, it was difficult to like her children when they reached their late adolescence. Difficult to like them: the pathos of the expression, the real suffering of it, makes me want to weep the world away, to quote the poet Shelley.

So Jesus was frustrated. The lesson should not be lost on us. At times we are so impatient with others; Christ also had impatience, apparently especially with those who were closest to him. In this, as in all things, the Word-made-flesh reveals a measure of humanity: the aching awareness of the failures of others to understand that can take one to the edge of despair.

Like some of our frustrations, Christ's begins with what seems a casual, even trivial, thing. Wanting to warn his disciples about two extremes in the social currents of his time, he says, "Beware of the leaven of the Pharisees and the leaven of Herod" (Mark 8:15, *The New Greek-English Interlinear New Testament*). The Pharisees were the spiritual leaders who pretended to ultimate religious authority as the Herodians did to political power.

Both movements were formidable. We tend to discount the Herodians out of ignorance of their brief success not ten years after the death of Christ (A.D. 41-44), when the miserable Agrippa was made king of Judea and Samaria. This meant that for a moment a formally Jewish State was granted an unusual degree of autonomy within the Roman Empire. It also meant open persecution of Christians in Palestine. This regime dissolved with the horrible death of Herod Agrippa (recounted in Acts 12:20-23) and the return to the Roman prefecture in Judea, one more step on the road to the fateful Jewish revolution against the Empire, which concluded with the destruction of Jerusalem.

We can sometimes also forget about the tremendous success of the Pharisee movement. Even in the time of Christ, the people tended to be more impressed with the Pharisees than they ought to have been. They were religious bullies without a sense of the mercy of God but somehow managed to make nearly everyone see their "righteousness" as a measure of religion. Their success over rival movements in Judaism was inevitable after the fall of Jerusalem and the dissolution of the Temple and all cultic sacrifice.

The warnings of Christ seem to have been in vain for the majority of people of his time. They nearly were for his disciples, who thought that he was talking about why they had forgot to take more bread with them on the boat. The contrast between the historic and intellectual concerns reflected in Jesus' admonition, which we can translate as "Beware the influence of two movements that represent opposite but mistaken paths for God's people," and the disciples' panic about not taking provisions, is comic.

It is one of the characteristics of St. Mark's portrait of the "duh"-sciples that they nearly always give the wrong answer to Jesus. They have a knack of getting things wrong, sometimes like this, in a way we can compare to television comedians, like the famous Roseanna Roscannadanna skits from *Saturday Night Live*. "Uh-oh, he's talking about leaven; he must have guessed we only have one loaf of bread on board," is a totally inappropriate way to respond to the dramatic warning that Jesus was giving. No wonder he loses his patience in a torrent of questions. Like me with my ninth graders, he seems exasperated.

I cannot help thinking about how I exasperate the Lord. In his questions here to the disciples, I can hear him talking to me: "Why do you so consistently miss the point? Don't you remember? Is your heart hardened? Do you not yet understand?"

The scholastics saw intellectual operations in terms of memory, understanding, and will. St. Ignatius of Loyola used memory, understanding, and will in his famous exercises to guide a Christian to personal liberation in Jesus. I see these elements in the string of questions we are reflecting about here.

"Don't you remember?" he says to me, and I have to think about how I forget what I sometimes preach to other people. *"Is your heart hardened?"* is about my will, which is inevitably related to understanding. I have to want to understand, or insight will not make its sometimes "bloody entrance," to quote a dramatic phrase from one of the most impenetrable Catholic philosophers of the last century. I have to ask myself, *"Do I yet not understand?"* I am afraid that I know the answer to that one.

Like the disciples in St. Mark, many of us seem to have an instinct for missing the point. Hearing this series of questions-reprimands from Jesus should chasten us and make us more humble. ◇

And when he had spit on his eyes and laid his hands upon him, he asked him, "Do you see anything?"   — Mark 8:23

Jesus asks this question during one of the more enigmatic of his miracles, recounted in Mark 8:22-26. When the Master arrives in Bethsaida, people bring a blind man to him. He grasped the blind man's hand and takes him outside the town. He then spits on the man's eyes, according to the literal Greek, reflected here (a more decorous translation says, "He put saliva on his eyes," which is not much better), and imposes hands on him. And then, "Do you see anything?"

Is this an example of the healing craft of Jesus? Was he saying, "Is that any better?" like the doctors do? I taught this passage once in a sixth grade religion class and asked for a summary. One boy gave me a very memorable one. The people had asked Jesus for the healing of the blind man, and so the Lord had blessed him. It didn't work the first time, so Jesus had to do it twice. The second try came out all right.

I remember being amused by the implication that even Jesus had experience of the adage "If at first you don't succeed, try, try again." It is another puzzling detail of the miracle, along with the taking of the man out of town, spitting in his eyes, and forbidding him to go back into the village. The fact that the man says that he sees men as though they were trees is not puzzling, because it implies that he had become blind and had not been born so. However, the few lines of the story do make me think.

If we do not accept that Jesus hadn't been able to make the man see clearly the first time, what do we say about this question? My idea is that he has given us here an example of process. The clarification of the man's vision, which involves the two impositions of hands, makes for a good metaphor about progress in the spiritual life.

Shortly after I was ordained, I heard a story about a priest who went to the shrine of Our Lady of Guadalupe to pray for a "second conversion." The brother priest who told me the story felt that the man who prayed for the second conversion had somehow decided his life in that way. Shortly after his pilgrimage, he took sick and had to move away from the diocese. The priest who told me the story thought that the sickness and its consequences had been the price of the second conversion.

Perhaps you have never heard of a second conversion. It does not imply a relapse to sin from a first conversion. According to an old classic of spiritual theology, Père Garrigou-Lagrange's *The Three Stages of Interior Life*, "In the lives of most saints and religious, there are ordinarily two conversions. One occurs when there is an offering of self to God, and the other when the person seeks the path of perfection."

The second conversion comes after the purification of the soul, which is called the *via purgativa* in the classical framework of spirituality, purgation-illumination-contemplation. The start of the "illumination" stage is a turning to greater perfection. The great spiritual writers could relate these stages and movement to the call of the apostles and their later development as disciples. First, the Lord called the apostles, and then much later they received the Holy Spirit. Jesus also says to St. Peter at the Last Supper, "I have prayed for you that your faith may not fail; and when you have turned again, strengthen your brethren" (Luke 22:32). The "turning again" of Peter was his second conversion, and this is seen in the lives of many saints.

The blind man at Bethsaida had a conversion in that he could "see men; but they look like trees, walking" (Mark 8:24). In other words, he had begun to discern but did not yet see things as they are. The second imposition of hands could be seen as the second conversion that clarifies vision. Our parallel with the blind man is interesting. We were brought to Jesus like him. We need a special experience with Jesus also, for him to touch us, to take us by the hand, and even to "leave the town" of our everyday lives and pre-occupations so that we can feel his power. We have had a communion with him that has given us some insight. But we still have a way to go before we can see clearly.

The question of Jesus to the blind man is thus a question for us. "Do you see anything?" Jesus asks us. How well are we seeing? He is well aware of our progress spiritually, but he asks us to make us more conscious of his work in us. "Is that better?" What is happening to you?

As a confessor for more than twenty years, I have had much occasion to see spiritual development in people. I have often seen a new depth of the awareness of sin in persons who have been growing spiritually. They remember sins that they had forgotten. They are keenly aware of faults against persons or of ingratitude to the Lord. They have gained perspective, and the difference is as great as seeing figures like trees and recognizing human beings. But discernment can take years, and conversion is a slow process, sometimes.

This question reminds us of Jesus' activity in that process. I tell him that I can see some things but that I still cannot discern well. He must touch me again, give me a renewal of his spirit by the imposition of his hands, so that I can be healed. And he must guide me, tell me not to return to my old sinful ways, as he told the blind man, "Do not even enter the village" (Mark 8:26). I know that he has called me to perfection, a call that I have been very slow in hearing.

What about your "second" conversion? That is where I see the utility of this question of Jesus for our reflection. "How well do you see?" he asks you. Perhaps it would be good to tell him, "I can see some things but not others." Then he will touch you again, and give you his vision. ◇

And Jesus went on with his disciples, to the villages of Caesarea
Philippi; and on the way he asked his disciples, "Who do men
say that I am?"   — Mark 8:27

I spent a memorable evening with a group of priests and a
very rich man in a mansion that overlooked the bay of
Acapulco, Mexico. A friend of mine had combined a trip to
Mexico with a visit to me in El Salvador, and had invited me to
accompany him on a visit to a former classmate who worked
in the Mexican province of his order. This priest was in charge
of fund-raising and development for the order in Mexico. He
worked very hard searching out financing for various major
projects, including seminaries and offices for the episcopal conference.

He was used to hobnobbing with high rollers and had been
able to extract money from them for many good works. The
visit of his friends and classmates, who were seminary professors and whom he had always admired, was an opportunity for
him to show off his own work and to treat them to the beauty
of Acapulco. Another rich man lent him a house on a great hill
that had a splendid view of the city and the bay. But the highlight was the visit to an even more splendid house further up
the hill and dinner with a very wealthy donor to the order,
who was also a close personal friend of the priest.

The man was very mysterious and talked about knowing
people and places around the world. He had made a fortune in
the development of real estate and tourism and was very well
connected. A congressman from Texas joined us for preprandial
drinks but had not been invited to dinner. The dinner was

fresh fish from the bay, prepared especially, and we ate at a great table in a garden.

So far, so good. Then the man decided to share with us that he had just read an interesting book about Jesus. It turned out that it was a cheap paperback that claimed to solve the mystery of the hidden life of Jesus, that is, from age twelve to thirty. Dives (I call him that because it is the traditional name given to the rich man in the parable of the poor man Lazarus) said that he had been surprised to learn that Jesus had learned secrets of the Tibetan monks and had studied with the magicians of Egypt. For him, the book was a revelation and he accepted all that it said.

As he detailed the "discoveries" of the book, which he had purchased in a drugstore, I could see that the professor's blood pressure was rising. Finally, he started to sputter out, "But that book is a bunch of nonsense. There is nothing scholarly about it. Why wouldn't the Scripture tell us about something that important concerning Jesus?"

Now the priest who was in charge of milking the rich for projects became very nervous. He respected his friend and classmate, but he didn't want Dives offended. Dives looked surprised that anyone would doubt his dime-store theology text, so his priest friend hastened to say, "Well, we can't know anything about it anyway. What would it matter if Jesus had studied in Egypt and the Himalayas? There is a right to speculate. Why can't there be speculation?"

His friend didn't think so, and it took some doing before the subject was dropped. I must confess I was amused at the panic it caused the fund-raiser to see his friend the theologian arguing very forcefully with his friend the benefactor. I think I will always remember the look of fear on his face when he realized that things were not going so smoothly at the dinner. The threat of losing future contributions had intruded on our private dinner party in the lap of luxury, and it scared the priest who had organized the whole thing. I have never been envious of those whose task it is to coddle the rich into giving some money away. It can be very hard work.

The rich man had been telling us who he thought Jesus was. It was an idea that was something out of fantasy, but it obviously worked for him. It horrified the professional theologians present, while it amused me and made the fund-raiser very nervous. I am reminded of the scene now because Jesus asks his disciples who do people say that he is.

"The people" — a generic enough title for others, I suppose — thought many things. One could even say that the ideas were more far-fetched than that of the Tibetan novitiate of Jesus or his postgraduate work among the magicians of Egypt. "The people," said the disciples, thought that Jesus was John the Baptist *redivivus*, come back from the dead to continue his work, or else Elijah or one of the other prophets.

The Gospels say that even Herod the Tetrarch entertained the notion that Jesus might be John the Baptist back from the dead. The idea does not fit with any other Old Testament notions we can see but shows how the ministry of the two men could be identified in the public mind. The prophecy of the return of Elijah is something that we can see in the Scripture and one that Jesus himself addressed at one point. That, after all, was in the book of the prophet Malachi: "Behold, I will send you Elijah the prophet before the great and terrible day of the LORD comes" (Malachi 4:5). It is still puzzling, however, why "the people" seemed to see Jesus as someone else returned, instead of a new messenger from God.

It is not surprising, however, that people could get Jesus wrong. People (including yours truly and — if I may be bold — you yourself) are still getting Jesus wrong. We make him out to be somebody else.

Jesus was a prophet, say many non-Christians, but not the Son of God. What is more worrisome to me is that we who say that he is Lord don't seem to act on our belief. We might as well think he is John the Baptist if we only want to select some of the themes of his teaching for our meditation. He could be Elijah for all the worship we give him, or some other prophet for all the difference he makes in our lives. If he really is what we say he is, then why isn't our conduct very different?

I can take this question of Jesus and make a kind of survey of wrong answers about Jesus. There are many ideas about him floating around that are clearly wrong. The Congregation of Faith was severely criticized when investigations were made about certain theologians and their teachings about Jesus. There were people even in Catholic seminaries who seemed to think that we should have a *laissez faire* sort of approach to doctrine. A professor of mine characterized this attitude as, "Let a thousand flowers bloom." A sociologist not connected to the Church made a commentary I appreciated at the time. If doctrine is a matter of indifference, then it is not even worth discussing. The theologians, he said, should welcome the investigation of their work because they are seeking the truth in community. They should want to be taken seriously on the highest level, said the sociologist, because that is what they are about: an expression of the whole community, not particular and peculiar ideas.

I cannot forget that it is possible to get Jesus wrong and that I must work very hard to get him right. That is why we need to correct constantly our ideas about Jesus in terms of the teaching of the Church. We are living in an age in which the decline of doctrine is so accepted it is sometimes celebrated. If we really believe, however, we have to want to believe in the objective truth. That is why the *Catechism of the Catholic Church* is so important: The truth about Jesus is not just a string of quotations from the Bible; it has to be synthesized, and the only synthesis that is guaranteed is that of the Church.

If my ideas about Jesus are to count, they have to be the same as those of the Church. Otherwise, I can be like "the people" of the time of Jesus, holding my own personal version of who he is: something that is a product of my ignorance or preferences. I don't want to fall into the category of those whose ideas about Jesus are only their own dime-store versions of him, like the paperback revelations of my friends in Mexico. Such ideas are more fantasy than substance — more about me than about Jesus. ◇

"But who do you say that I am?" Peter answered, "You are the Christ." And he charged them to tell no one about him.

— Mark 8:29-30

The Greek word for a teacher who instructed his listeners as he wandered from place to place (literally, walking around) is the root of the English word "peripatetic." The great philosopher Socrates did not teach in lecture halls but in the most informal of settings. Jesus was an even more peripatetic teacher than Socrates, walking and talking apparently the whole length of the Palestine of his time. This question and the one before it constitute one of Jesus' lesson plans in their moving classroom.

It is worth thinking about the site of the lesson a bit. Some years ago, I visited the ruins of Caesarea Philippi in the northeast corner of the State of Israel, a territory not far from the Lebanese and Syrian borders. Christians go to the place because it is the site of the profession of Peter. The Druse, a sect that derives in some way from Islam, has some connection with the spot also. People interested in antiquity are interested in Banias (as Caesarea Philippi appears on Israeli maps) because of the remains of a pagan temple with votary niches to the Greek god Pan. The lack of a church on the spot means that one has to reflect in open air about the very important lesson the Lord gave here to his disciples.

Why did the Lord choose the place to talk about a central truth of his mission? Banias was not part of Galilee and was ruled by Herod's brother Philip. After the death of Herod the Great, their father, his lands had been divided up among his heirs. King Herod the Great (it is important to keep straight the various men who have the same name) had built a temple in honor of Caesar Augustus in the city that had been called Paneas. His son Philip, not a king but a "tetrarch" (ruler of a fourth) like his brother Herod, had changed the name of the city to Caesarea, trying vainly to outdo his father in sycophancy, perhaps. However, since there was another Caesarea, which actually had been built by his father, *his* city carried the modifying "Philippi," Philip's Caesarea.

The city had a history and a kind of symbolic ambience. First, there was the Greek culture evident in the devotion to Pan. Then there was the Roman imperial association. Caesarea was perhaps not so large, but it was an outpost of the far-flung Roman Empire, with all the symbolism that the world's mightiest government up to that time could evoke. A Jewish king had committed the sin of constructing there a temple in honor of the emperor. It was perhaps one of the more transparent moments in which King Herod revealed his true religion, the worship of power. Jesus and his disciples would have felt the strangeness of the place spiritually. Although this was the ancient territory of the tribe of Dan, and right near Mount Hermon, which had so many biblical associations, Jesus was in pagan country, where false gods and emperors were worshiped.

The cult of Pan must have been shocking for the Jews. He was a minor deity for the Greeks, a god that was represented as part goat and part man. He played music, was constantly falling in love with the woodland nymphs, and always rejected because of his ugliness. Pan was a strange deity, mischievous at times and perhaps a bit cruel. From his name derives the notion of "panic," and many travelers who heard noises in the night as they were camped on the side of roads would attribute their uneasiness to the god's capriciousness.

In the midst of paganism, in a society that knew not God, at the far corner of biblical Israel, near the holy mountain Hermon, Jesus asked his disciples who they thought he was.

The relationship between Jesus and the apostles was certainly mysterious. It is evident in this scene that the disciples were not sure what to say. Some people live with more ambiguity than others do — for instance, in relationships. I think that the ambiguity the disciples lived must have been tension-producing. Was he the Messiah? When would his time come? What relationship will we have with him when he ascends to power? All these questions were apparently unspoken. The Gospel tells us that there were questions the disciples were afraid to ask.

I imagine that after the previous question, "Who do people say that I am?" there was a sense of expectation in the small group in Philip's Caesarea. When Jesus asks, "And who do you say that I am?" I think there may have been some discomfort. For all the ambiguity of their relationship with Jesus, I am sure that the disciples had intense feelings about him. If at times they did not dare ask him a question, they most certainly didn't want to get it wrong when he asked them a question. It is no surprise that St. Peter, the most impulsive, is the one who answers the interrogative. His was the valor of his sincerity.

It is almost painful to see how the story unfolds. Peter is right and knows that he is. In St. Matthew, Christ praises him, saying, "Blessed are you, Simon Bar-Jona, for flesh and blood did not reveal this to you" (Matthew 16:17, *The New Greek-English Interlinear New Testament*), and goes on to say that Peter is the rock foundation of the Church. St. Mark only says that Jesus warned the disciples not to tell anyone that he was the Messiah. With the ambiguity of whether he was the Messiah resolved now, Jesus introduces yet another ambiguity: that he is the secret Messiah, and no one is to know.

Being a disciple of Jesus must have been a confusing proposition. Actually, it still is for us. There is always some ambiguity about our faith. We cannot understand what the Lord is doing all the time, or he wouldn't be Lord. We are asked to accept that he is our Savior, but at times he certainly seems to be taking his good old time saving us. He still is a secret Savior in some respects, because there is a level of life in which we cannot see his activity clearly.

Many of us are in a kind of Caesarea Philippi in our own heads. We live in the midst of a culture that — although, like the biblical city, it lives in the shadows of a holy mountain, the Christian tradition of the previous centuries — is more pagan than not. Superstition abounds, even while faith declines, so we cannot judge too harshly the votaries of the goat-boy god. Did we not have the relatively recent example of a Christian president arranging his calendar by astrology? Nor can we criticize too strongly the Roman practice of worshiping the Caesars. The powerful are still worshiped in our midst. I remember being appalled by a good Catholic who had been pleased to have been able to shake the hand of the man solely responsible for allowing the barbaric practice of partial-birth abortion to continue in our country. We worship power and celebrity in our culture. We live in the vortex of so many strange currents of ideas and ideologies that we sometimes don't even realize the strangeness of our own thoughts.

And Jesus says to us, "Who do you say that I am?" What do you say? ◇

"For what does it profit a man, to gain the whole world and forfeit his life? For what can a man give in return for his life?"
— Mark 8:36-37

I can remember the first time Juan talked to me seriously. It was after a session of the youth group and I had to take a number of the young people home because they lived on the outskirts of the village. There is some kind of law about pastoral work that correlates the worst time for someone to want to talk with a priest with the most urgent need. Many times I am late — on my way to something I, at least, think urgent — and a person comes to drop in my lap some terrible crisis, or confess a sin he has been carrying around for years. It is like the observation that life is what happens while you think you are going to get something done for a change.

Juan said that he had wanted to talk for some time. His parents had told him that his absence at the youth meetings had made me ask for him. He had been sick. Actually, he had been sick for most of his life, something he thought had come about because as a young boy he had fallen from a tree. Some had thought that he had died in the accident, because he had been unconscious for a long time. He was thin, and he showed me his arms. "I have never been able to put on weight," he said. Juan had been in and out of hospitals since the near-fatal accident, although I was never sure exactly about what his problem was.

He suffered from asthma, among other things. His parents, who were simple people who had never studied, said that he needed injections of potassium every once in a while. The care of the sick was so uneven in the country that it would be hard to say whether the doctors would have been able to explain his situation any better. At any rate, his illness was something that Juan was used to thinking about. "I know that I am going to die young," Juan said to me with a matter-of-fact tone of voice that surprised me.

"*No, hombre*," I said, which is the vernacular for "No way, man." I told him that he had to think positively. He was only twenty-one years old, after all. There was always hope. If he had the wrong attitude, how could he get stronger?

The only response to this was a nod. Juan really wanted to talk about something else. In a matter of minutes, we dived into some of the terrible experiences he had had, some of which he had seen as insuperable problems for his life with God. We celebrated a quick sacrament of reconciliation in the garden next to the unused priest's house in the village, in the semi-darkness, while the other members of the group waited for us at the door, some already standing in the back of the pickup.

It was vacation time and so we had many walking excursions with the group. He accompanied us on some of them, sometimes walking partway and getting a ride for the return, because he was not very strong. One day we climbed a very high hill, and I stopped by to see whether he wanted to walk with us, but he didn't feel up to it. After the summer vacation, I was transferred, and Juan was present at various farewell activities people in his town organized for me. Each time we saw each other we would be able to talk seriously but briefly. He told me that he had a girlfriend, but that she was going to the United States, sent for by relatives who were residents. He declined to give her name.

I was really sorry to say good-bye to him as well as to the others in the group. One of my problems is that I am never very detached emotionally from my parishes. I would miss him, I said. He looked as though he would cry but contained himself. He had told me more than perhaps anyone of what he had seen, done, and felt. With his nature, I knew that it would be hard for him to cover the same ground with anyone else. I had the intention of keeping up, because the other parish was only a few hours away. We would see each other again.

It didn't turn out that way. The new parish was consuming, there was a national emergency because of earthquakes, and I had to make an unplanned trip abroad. The first news I had about Juan was a call at ten o'clock at night from a friend who said that he had been released from the hospital and was dying at home. I said I would try to come the next day. He died that night at two in the morning. The next day I made it to his wake at ten o'clock at night.

Seeing him in his casket was a shock to me. He looked as if he were asleep, and I actually whispered some words to him, like a crazy person or a character in a movie. His parents told me that he had asked for me in the hospital and had smiled when told that I had spoken with his friend on the phone. There are experiences in life that feel like you just got clobbered. You think, where did this come from, how could I have avoided it? This was one of them for me.

There is a phrase by the Latin poet Virgil that describes the sadness that life brings sometimes: *lacrimae rerum*, "the tears of things that have happened." *Lacrimae rerum* were in my eyes in the crowded room that day, and everyone seemed to be watching my reaction. I thought of how the people watched Jesus as he wept at the grave of Lazarus and said, "See how much he loved him!"

Despite the example of Jesus, priests are not really given a lot of room for private grief. I had to do a kind of "I'll cry tomorrow" routine and we had a celebration of the word that lasted until about eleven o'clock. The next morning, at seven, we celebrated Juan's funeral and three hours later I was at work in my office in the capital.

I don't even have a photo of Juan. My grief for him had the backdrop of a very pagan notion that must lurk in the shadows of my consciousness: "Is that all there is?" My reflection about him, my regret that I did not see him before he died, my wish to see him again — all must be for a purpose, however. Jesus is telling me something about life, not just Juan's, but my life, too.

The word in Greek that is translated "life" in this text is *psyche*, a word which could also be translated as "soul." My meditation on Juan's death makes me favor this other translation. *What can a man give in return for his soul?* St. John Chrysostom, in the *Catena Aurea*, is cited as saying, "For a man can give the price of his house in exchange for the house, but in losing his soul he has not another soul to give."

I have no fear that Juan lost his soul, because he had a holy death, supported by the sacraments and the prayers of friends around the simple cot where he accepted death's embrace. What consoles me is to think that *although he did not gain the world, in spite of a life that was frustrating and sad,* Juan's soul is with God. The soul is the principle of life that endures beyond our present existence. Thoughts of the soul logically give us the capacity to transcend the temptations and trials of this life, to see things *sub specie aeternitatis*, "with the perspective of eternity."

The great English poet Tennyson wrote his noble poem "In Memoriam A.H.H.," which was about the death of his friend Arthur Henry Hallam. In the conclusion of the poem Tennyson speaks of "that friend of mine that lives in God." The phrase can apply to any number of deceased friends and relatives, and they can remind us, as "In Memoriam" declares, of "one far-off divine event / To which the whole creation moves," that is, our future with God.

Our own movement toward God is helped by the reflection on the importance of our soul. This question of Jesus might be in the secret ear of our consciousness as we kneel next to the casket of a loved one. May we give it consideration before someone else is kneeling beside our remains. ◇

And he said to them, "Elijah does come first to restore all things; and how is it written of the Son of man, that he should suffer many things and be treated with contempt?"
— Mark 9:12

There are public questions that are inescapable at times. Everybody seems to have an opinion about them, and those who have not seen CNN are inclined not to make their ignorance about the subject known. Who was not talking about what happened or was to happen in the presidential elections in Florida in 2000, for instance? I think the same was true to an even more penetrating level in discussions about the Messiah in first-century Palestine. Everyone must have had an idea about when the Messiah was to come and how he was to go about the business of redeeming the Jews.

This had to be something discussed in every synagogue in the country with a great deal of passion and many varieties of positions and principles. The question was so important that it had to be on everyone's mind, even for those who did not necessarily want the Messiah to come, like King Herod as he is presented in St. Matthew. I am sure that the details of the prophecies about the Messiah were a kind of obsession for the men who gathered in the synagogues and debated close readings of the prophets and other biblical texts in the rabbinical style.

The prophecy about Elijah is found in Malachi, which tells us: "Behold, I will send you Elijah the prophet before the great and terrible day of the LORD comes. And he will turn the hearts of the fathers to their children and the hearts of the children to their fathers, lest I come and smite the land with a curse" (Malachi 4:5-6).

Jesus gives an interpretation of this verse that is far from literal. "Elijah does come first," he says. In St. Matthew, what the Lord intends to say by this is much clearer:

> He replied, "Elijah does come, and he is to restore all things; but I tell you that Elijah has already come, and they did not know him, but did to him whatever they pleased. So also the Son of man will suffer at their hands." Then the disciples understood that he was speaking to them of John the Baptist.   — Matthew 17:11-13

In the Gospel of St. Mark we are told that Jesus has just come down from the mountain following his Transfiguration, in which Elijah was present. He doesn't bother to talk about the Baptist here, because the real issue appears to be the association between the prophecy of Elijah and the necessity of the suffering Messiah. That was not a concept with great currency, since most felt that the Messiah would walk to power without any contretemps.

The Navarre Bible has a helpful gloss on this: "The scribes and Pharisees interpret the messianic prophecy in Malachi 3:1-2 as meaning that Elijah will appear in person, dramatically, to be followed by the all-triumphant Messiah, with no shadow of pain or humiliation. Jesus tells them that Elijah has indeed come, in the person of John the Baptist and has prepared the way of the Messiah, a way of pain and suffering" (*The Navarre Bible: St. Mark's Gospel*, Four Courts Press, 1992).

The scribes and Pharisees had it wrong not only about the Elijah prophecy but also about the Messiah whose triumph would be revealed only in apparently agonizing defeat. Jesus is responding here to the disciples' question (inspired perhaps by their having seen Elijah with the Lord on Mount Tabor) "Why do the scribes say that Elijah must come first?" This question of the disciples was no doubt very important for them. If Jesus was the Messiah, then what about the key prophecy concerning Elijah? Their faith in Jesus depended in some way on the doubt about this element. Jesus practically dismisses the question by reaching beyond it to the question about the suffering of the Son of man.

Sometimes we tell children or young people, "You will not understand what I am saying now, but later you will know why." Jesus tried very hard to prepare his disciples for his violent death, but they could not understand what he was talking about. This was another attempt to steer their thinking to the suffering Messiah.

My own response to this question is not so much concerned with its original intention of making the disciples see that the scribes did not understand many things. I think of the question in absolute terms. Why did the Son of man have to suffer? Why did God's intervention to save us have to be so violent? Why were we saved by bloodshed?

Violence is a great part of life where I live right now. El Salvador supposedly is the most violent society after Haiti in this hemisphere. There are few weeks in which I do not hear about terrible acts of violence. Just recently, one of our leaders came to me to talk about an experience that made me feel intensely the precariousness of life here and the insecurity.

He had to work a night shift and had slept all afternoon. As a confirmed bachelor — very rare here — he decided to grab something to eat in a small restaurant that he knew would be open late. He was still outside of the establishment when he heard an altercation happening within. There was a fight going on that continued on to the sidewalk across the street, a half a block from where he watched, hidden by a tree. He saw a man he recognized as a member of a local gang cruelly beating another whom he knew as somebody constantly in trouble for his insults and aggressive speech. Eventually the gang member grabbed a piece of concrete that was at hand and smashed it against the other's skull.

As my friend watched the murder, he had been gripped by a paralyzing fear. As he told me this, tears formed in the corners of his eyes and his voice broke. The worst for him was that he had been called into questioning by the police, who had somehow learned that he had been in the area of the crime. In El Salvador protection of witnesses is nonexistent. The other gang members would see to it that he suffered if he were to be a witness in a trial. What could he do?

He was not the only witness. The owner of the restaurant and another friend of the deceased had seen the crime. I went to the prosecutor, a friend of a priest friend of mine, and he worked it out that the witness would only be called upon if there were no other way. The moral obligation to be a witness was more problematic if he were the only one who could help. The prosecutor understood the fears of our pastoral agent. The solution was acceptable to all of us.

I cannot forget, however, the tension in his voice as he told me about seeing the violence, the fear that I could read in his usually jovial face as he said he had no idea what he could do. Would I tell him to endanger himself? I think he really wanted to hear himself talk than to hear what I would say. The trauma he suffered was so palpable, it was as if another person were in the room with us.

One of the Bible quotes that has always puzzled me is this one: "And from the days of John the Baptist until now, the kingdom of heaven suffereth violence, and the violent bear it away" (Matthew 11:12, *Douay-Rheims Bible*). I cannot help thinking that my friend hiding behind a tree witnessing a brutal murder is the kingdom of heaven suffering violence. But what can it mean that "the violent bear it away," the words the profound American Catholic writer Flannery O'Connor used for a title of one of her novels?

Why did our Savior have to suffer violence? Surely this is part of the mystery here. This violent world required a Messiah who suffered violence. That is something I have learned living in a country where the violence is less hidden than it is in the States. The history of the insecurity of human life across the planet — something we live now with all the disadvantages of technology — is the story of an all-consuming violence that could not respect even the Son of God.

The question "Why did the Messiah have to suffer?" is part of the mystery of the cosmos and is unanswerable. However, asking it, we can absorb some wisdom. It leads us to the question "And is our suffering part of the same?" ◇

"What are you discussing with them?"   — Mark 9:16

I have visited Mount Tabor two times. The Church of the Transfiguration, which stands on the summit of the mountain, is for me the most beautiful in the Holy Land. I suppose that it is because of the spiritual ambience of the shrine. High on the mountain, it is a place apart, where it is easy to think of one's spirit lifting up to heaven. The spectacular view, the well-landscaped grounds, the absence of vendors, and the lack of hustling with other pilgrims that disturbs the tranquillity in so many of the most sacred places of our religion make Tabor a very special place.

On both visits, I did not want to leave. I found myself fantasizing about making a long retreat there on the mountain. Maybe this is only an echo of these words of St. Peter: "Master, it is well that we are here; let us make three booths, one for you and one for Moses and one for Elijah" (Mark 9:5). Whatever it is, even as I write this I feel a desire to be on that mountain again and to drink in the air of contemplation.

The Scripture says that Peter suggested building the shelters because "he did not know what to say" (Mark 9:6). I think I know what he had to say, however. The itinerant preaching of Jesus must have been hard work. At the miracle of the multiplication of the loaves one gets the impression that the disciples wanted more time alone with the Lord. The ministry of Jesus, which was also their ministry, got in the way of the relationship of the disciples with the Lord. I feel sometimes that my ministry to others takes away my time with the Lord, too. Our hearts need to find rest in the Lord, and sometimes it seems that only completely apart from our ordinary lives will we have a chance to be with him.

That is why we need especially intense moments of prayer, retreats, and days of recollection. These fill our hearts and make us remember who and why we are. But then life comes crashing in again. At least that is my experience, and I sense that it was the same for the Lord. Directly down from the mountain, Jesus and the three disciples who experienced the Transfiguration encounter the other disciples in the middle of an argument with some scribes. The people, who were evidently following the discussion as spectators, were so happy to see Jesus arrive that they "ran" to him. Was this because they liked a good fight?

Jesus has just come down from the tranquillity of Tabor, where he was transfigured in the glory of his communion with the Father. His first experience after that glory is conflict. The scribes, who resented his teaching, were no doubt getting the best of his disciples, who were not learned men. A short trip down the mountain, and Jesus is in the thick of it again. St. Peter's moment of peace was over.

Jesus asks his disciples, "What are you arguing with them?" This is the more literal meaning of the Greek word translated by the *Revised Standard Version* as "discussing." It is interesting that the disciples do not answer the Lord. Instead, the man whose problem had caused the controversy speaks up. His son is possessed by a mute spirit, and he asked that the disciples of Jesus would cure him. However, he says, the disciples "were not able" (Mark 9:18).

What were they all arguing about, then? That Jesus must not be the Messiah because his disciples could not do the exorcism? Did the disciples have the presence of mind to challenge the scribes to do what they could not? I don't know if this is too personal a reading, but I detect in Jesus' question to the disciples an insinuation that the argument was not useful.

"What is going on here?" is my understanding of what Jesus wants to know. What has caused this situation to get out of hand?

Jesus concludes that the problem had to do with a lack of faith, but that is the reflection about the question that immediately follows this one. Nevertheless, we can profit by listening to the words in our hearts: "What are you arguing about?"

Doesn't Jesus catch me off guard with that question when I get involved in problems and disputes that are far from the core of the message that I must give to others? Don't I sometimes get entangled in discussions that do not speak of faith but rather of the lack of it? Aren't some things left better for his immediate intervention rather than for my own words? Wouldn't the disciples have been better off saying, "Wait for our Master," and not speculating on other things?

Many times our "discussions" can be without value because the only thing we can do is refer the case to Jesus himself. He has to be the absolute center of our lives. We complicate sometimes the most essential questions. We have to remember: Jesus is the only solution to our problems. I don't mean this to be the escapist way favored by some of the evangelists of cheap grace that plague our times. There is one pastor in El Salvador who says that his true believers will never suffer even financial reverses because Jesus "solves everything." The only solution is faith in the crucified One who will deliver us from death, even though we have to pass through a kind of crucifixion ourselves. Whatever challenges we have or crosses we bear, we need a deep faith.

One of the great lessons I have received from working with the poor is to see how God penetrates every aspect of their lives. We who are better off tend to compartmentalize our lives. There is a section for God, although many times it is extremely reduced. Then there are sections for our relationships, our work, our interests, and even our emotional needs. With the poor in

El Salvador, there are few compartments. Everything has to do with everything else and, more importantly, with God. The phrase used very frequently in conversation, *Primero Dios* (literally "God first," but with the meaning "If God wills it so" or even "May God will it so"), is an indication that God is always the point of reference.

In the United States, people say, "Oh God," but they are very often not referring all things to the Divine Being. The very casualness of the references made to God is an index of our lack of faith. That reminds me of another index of devotion: Are children in the States still taught to bow their heads at the mention of the name of Jesus? In fact, I don't know. I do know, however, that we could all use more focusing on God.

That is what I "take home" with me from reflection on this question of Jesus. While I am discussing, I should be waiting for him. I cannot escape the impression that sometimes I get lost in words when what I really need is to just wait for Jesus to take the matter in hand. I imagine the disciples a bit abashed at the scene, their inadequacy is underscored by their later asking Jesus "in private" why they had not been able to cast out the demon. His answer — that only prayer could cast out "this kind" of demon — points out that our lives are part of the divine mystery and only by union with God can we do some things. If I focus on what I can do, I will be just as frustrated as the disciples were.

And likewise with you. Jesus may be asking you, "What are you arguing about?" ◇

"O faithless generation, how long am I to be with you? How long am I to bear with you?" — Mark 9:19

This is obviously related to Question 17, "Why does this generation seek a sign?" Here Jesus is more forceful, however, adding the epithet "faithless" generation. What strikes me most is the impatience expressed in "How long am I to be with you? How long am I to bear with you?" There are many beautiful images and paintings that portray vividly the sufferings of Jesus, from the agony in the garden to the crucifixion. I would like to have one of Jesus' face when he asks these two related questions.

In that picture we would be asked to imagine the suffering implicit in the Incarnation even before Holy Week, when the physical sufferings of Jesus were extreme. Jesus' presence on earth, this world with so little faith, was also a part of his Passion, a word that is little understood now but comes from the Latin *passio*, suffering. How could an artist indicate the invisible suffering of Christ, a suffering that was self-imposed but not less difficult for that?

The Passion and death of Jesus we all know. It has been carved and painted by some of the greatest artists who have ever lived. The Passion in life is what this question can make us meditate upon. Jesus felt his life on earth as something to be endured. *How long am I to bear with you?* The thought should give us a deeper insight in the self-emptying of Jesus (the Greek word for this is *kenosis*) and how much sacrifice it meant. I wonder how an artist could render the anguish of the Savior who knew that the saved weren't so interested in rescue.

St. Paul quotes what must have been a current hymn about Jesus in the second chapter of Philippians: "Christ Jesus, who, though he was in the form of God, did not count equality with God a thing to be grasped, but emptied himself, taking the form of a servant, being born in the likeness of men. And being found in human form he humbled himself and became obedient unto death, even death on a cross" (Philippians 2:5-8).

Obviously Jesus' death was the final indignity and the sacrifice of his body in some way a consummation of the Incarnation. But Philippians allows us to think that all of "the days of his flesh [that is, Jesus' flesh]," as the letter to the Hebrews calls the earthly ministry (cf. Hebrews 5:7), were days of sacrifice. Jesus not only humbled himself, says the great Swiss theologian Hans Urs von Balthasar, he *humiliated* himself, exposing his person to all "the heart-ache and the thousand natural shocks / that flesh is heir to" (*Hamlet*, III.i.56).

The letter to the Hebrews talks about the sacrifice of Christ's body:

> Consequently, when Christ came into the world, he said,
> "Sacrifice and offerings thou hast not desired,
>   but a body hast thou prepared for me;
> in burnt offerings and sin offerings thou hast
>   taken no pleasure.
> Then I said, 'Lo, I have come to do thy will,
>   O God.' "
>
> — Hebrews 10:5-7

Perhaps the first thing that comes to our mind here is the sacrifice on the cross, when Jesus gave his body over to cruel death for our sake. However, perhaps we can think of the sacrifice of the body as more extended in Christ's ministry.

One of our Scripture professors in the seminary gave us this example to meditate upon. He said that the Divine Being of Jesus was put into a kind of voluntary straitjacket because of the Incarnation. The all-powerful made himself powerless for us. The professor asked us to think of the consciousness of a young athletic man at the height of his strength entering the body of a seventy-year-old quadriplegic. All the capacities the young man had would be forfeited. His mobility would be constricted to the point where raising a spoon to his mouth would be equivalent in difficulty of running a fifty-yard touchdown.

"Imagine the patience that would require," said the professor. "The tremendous restriction of the flesh wedded to Divine Being required an infinite patience." The example has stayed with me longer than many proffered by seminary lecturers. For me, it describes an aspect of the Incarnation that we should never forget. When Jesus accepted becoming flesh for us, it was not only his death that he was accepting. He was saying "yes" to all the limitations and weaknesses of the flesh.

Obviously, as the Roman poet Horace said, *Omnia metaphora claudicat* ("All comparisons limp"). However, the value of this metaphor is to sense the disproportion between the mind of the young athlete and the body of the old and paralyzed man. In fact, accidents can happen that reduce the young and vigorous to paralysis, and the transformation is also dramatic. The point of the example of the young athlete inserted in the body of an old and paralyzed body, however, is the voluntary giving up of strength to live another kind of life. There is a certain violence of metaphor here, but it is useful. When the Word became flesh, he made possible the impossible: God who is beyond all suffering could now suffer.

And part of that suffering was rejection. For many people, emotional suffering is far worse than anything else. I know people who say that they would prefer sickness to abandonment. Shakespeare's King Lear said that the ingratitude of a child was "sharper than a serpent's tooth." A woman with cancer told me, "This I can handle. What I cannot get over is how my son has forgotten me."

Jesus' question here, "How long am I to bear with you?" proves that God suffered emotional pain. There are so many paradoxes that can be said because of the Incarnation. We can say, for instance, that God died on a cross. Certainly a paradox for our age is that God in Jesus knew what emotional suffering is. He felt rejection and frustration. I have known many co-workers experience burnout in their ministry. They sometimes don't get around to saying, "How long am I to bear with you?" — but they should be able to relate to what Jesus is expressing here.

Emotional pain is obviously linked to our bodies. Many psychosomatic conditions attest to that, as do stories of cures and returns to health. Many times emotional suffering is translated by our bodies into stomachaches and migraines, and it is a common belief that stress can cause or exacerbate certain types of cancer. The confusion emotions cause in us is related to our being flesh. Jesus was flesh, too. He did not bear the effects of original sin, as we do, and so I do not think he suffered "confusion"; but I do see in the Scripture evidence that he was anxious, that he was sad, that he felt alienation. This passage shows the alienation, the emotional distance, he felt from his contemporaries.

My own experience of alienation helps me to understand what Christ is expressing here, but I have to go beyond that. It is a constant in the biographies of the greatest saints that they were very conscious of their sinfulness. I, who am so far from being a saint, must see that I am a part of the faithless generation. I am one who makes the Lord say, "How long must I bear with you?" My own experience of faithlessness in others and the inevitable secret solitude that each one of us lives helps give me a light to this question. The Lord is asking me how long I will still wander from his ways, when I will finally bend my will to his.

An older religious language talked about how our sins added to the pains of the crucified Christ, sometimes with a detail that makes us uncomfortable now. We no longer say that our sins are more lashes that he received or more slaps in the face. Nevertheless, the insight that our lack of faith and love has to do with the torments of the Passion can be seen clearly in this question of Christ. How long will you and I frustrate Our Lord and Savior?

How long will the Lord bear with me? The question echoes down the corridors of history with a frightful resonance. ◇

And Jesus asked [the boy's] father, "How long has he had this?"   — Mark 9:21

The Roman poet Virgil in the *Aeneid* includes a maxim, *ab uno disce omnes*, that I think applies to this question. Literally the words mean, "from one learn all," with the sense that one case can help one understand all others. This is dangerous as a general principle but certainly can be true about some details. It is like the Russian proverb the great Aleksandr Solzhenitsyn wrote as an epigraph to his monumental *Gulag Archipelago*, "To have an idea of what the sea tastes like, one mouthful is sufficient."

This is a personal question of Jesus to a particular man in a particular circumstance, but it has universal relevance for us because it reveals how he related to people. We remember the context of this question from the previous reflection. When his disciples cannot exorcise the man's son, Jesus must do it himself. The demon, upon seeing Jesus close by, causes the boy he possesses to convulse and to throw himself on the ground and foam at the mouth. To paraphrase Mark 9:21, the Lord then asks a very human question: "How long has the boy suffered this way?"

In this simple inquiry I feel that we can sense some important things about Jesus. In the first place, his question reflects a very human reaction. He sees that the boy is violently ill and seeks to understand the experience of suffering involved, even if only by measuring it in time. This is terrible, he seems to imply. The question is not a clinician's interrogatory to fill out a sheet on a clipboard. It is about the father, too. How long have you, his father, had to suffer seeing this happening to him? Jesus engages the man in a dialog about how he has suffered with his son's sickness.

The man gives a reply that is heartrending. From childhood the boy has suffered this way, often dangerously, because he throws himself into water or fire. We can imagine the tremendous feeling of impotence of a father afraid that his child might destroy himself. I know several parents whose adolescent children have been diagnosed as suicidal. All are friends of mine, and I could sense the panic they felt that their children might do something to hurt themselves. Besides the guilt that immediately laid siege to them, they were quite simply (and quite naturally) frightened about what might happen to their children. Not unlike this man who (literally in the Greek) *runs* to Jesus with the problem of his son, they could feel that some power had taken over their sons or daughters. "She is not herself," one woman told me. "It is like dealing with another person."

It is easy for me to think of Jesus posing this question to each of my friends: "How long has this been happening to your child?" I imagine him relating to them, provoking them to tell their story, to indicate their grief, like the man in this passage of St. Mark. They, too, might be wondering why others have failed to cure their children. What about the school or church? Why didn't we notice; how come others could not tell us?

Nor is it difficult for me to think that a parent might have the doubts of the man who says, "But if you can do anything, have pity on us and help us" (Mark 9:22). Obviously this man had lost hope. Jesus seizes on that point and criticizes his choice of words: "If you can! All things are possible to him who believes" (Mark 9:23). Instantly the father says, "I believe; help my unbelief!" (Mark 9:24). This is like saying," I do believe, but I also doubt." The man's impetuous honesty is extremely sympathetic. I can easily imagine people I know saying the same thing.

Jesus' response to this statement of complicated faith is to heal the child. The deaf and dumb spirit is exorcised and the child "was like a corpse" (Mark 9:26), but then Jesus lifts him up. When his disciples ask Jesus how he did that, he responds somewhat mysteriously that nothing but prayer and fasting could drive such an evil spirit out. It is easy to see that the nineteen centuries that have passed since St. Mark's Gospel was written have left their stamp on our ideas about healing and demonic possession. What we would see as the curing of some kind of epilepsy, the Gospel calls an exorcism. Both expressions of the case are less than satisfactory, because one looks for the shortest path to the diagnosis of an illness and the other to seeing the healing as part of Christ's redemptive victory over the powers of darkness.

Nevertheless, in both cases, it is the power of Jesus that is posited, along with the importance of the power of faith. That is where I think this question of Jesus can be valuable for us. He first meets the man on the ground of his experience of the illness of his child. His question is echoed thousands of times in hospital corridors and doctors' consulting rooms. "When did this start?" it asks; but it really has a subtext, "How have you been able to take this?"

The applications of this type of relating of Jesus to us all are more extensive than to parents with confused teenagers. I think we all need to feel that the Lord takes an interest in the details of our life, especially the details of our suffering. We should feel encouraged by the gentle way he treats the man who had nearly run out of faith. While in the previous question Jesus seems almost irate asking about faith in a general way, in this specific case, he is very compassionate. He rejects the lack of faith, but rather than dwell on what is wrong, he calls for confidence in him.

I knew a priest who thought that his ministry called him to be a "lion in the pulpit but a lamb in the confessional." The two poles are evident in this question and the last. Jesus can lament very forcefully the lack of faith of a whole generation but only very mildly rebukes a concrete example of the same. The impatience of the exasperated question is replaced by the compassion of the gentle miracle worker, calling for stronger confidence in him.

This question is not a challenge to us, as others are in this Gospel. Rather it is a source of consolation. We should think of the Lord in dialog with us about whatever is difficult for us. He knows how long everything has been going on, but he works by process, just as we do. One of the psalms exhorts us to cast our cares upon the Lord, who cares for us (cf. Psalm 55:22). Tell Jesus how long you have suffered. He will expel the demons of destruction, especially self-destruction, and he will ask us to have more faith. ◇

"What were you discussing on the way?" — Mark 9:33

Saul Bellow has a short story collection with the amusing title *Him with His Foot in His Mouth, and Other Stories*. St. Mark's Gospel, which so often shows the fallible side of the disciples, could be entitled, *Them with Their Feet in Their Mouths, and Other Stories*. How many times does Jesus catch us the same way?

There is an anecdote about Winston Churchill, who was still in Parliament when he was in his eighties. A colleague knew it was the great leader's birthday and greeted him somewhat effusively. Churchill did not react very much, which led someone close by to say, "They say the old man is gaga." Churchill responded, "They say he's deaf, too." Needless to say, the joker regretted his joke.

We have all been there, to use a figure of speech that implies a comparison between experiencing something and visiting a place. Inopportunely, we have commented on a co-worker the moment he has come through the door or we have said something about a family member or friend when we did not know he or she could hear what we were saying.

In the case that prompts this question of Jesus, the disciples were discussing who was more important. This obviously tells us something about the ambiguity of the relationships between the disciples. At that point, at least, they had not yet gone beyond personal rivalries. The crucial problem with their debate, however, is its context.

Jesus and his disciples had been crossing Galilee practically in secret. St. Mark says the reason for the low profile was that the Master wanted to tell the apostles about the suffering and death that awaited him. This was the "bad news" of the Good News, the mystery of evil and the mystery of suffering. They didn't understand what he was telling them, however. Then the Scripture adds that they were afraid to ask for explanations. The fear tends to reveal the nature of their failure to understand. They don't ask because they really don't think they want to know. We do the same thing sometimes when we are afraid that we cannot really take the truth.

The reluctance to face the truth ironically makes company with an argument about who is more important. In the face of the bad news of the Good News, the apostles wanted to fight about their relative importance in the new dispensation of Jesus. They had totally missed the point the Master was making. Their ambition was a totally inadequate response to Christ's message of redemptive suffering.

And so is our ambition when put in the clear but sometimes harsh light of the Gospel. It is a reaction that is a cul-de-sac. Not only does it not further our journey, it will make us retrace our steps. Our petty desire to be more important than someone else distracts us from the real message of Christianity. By comparing ourselves with others, we forget that Jesus is the measure of all humanity, and that all relative measurements should make us humble. Those who are in competition with others even in what is good are following the Pharisee in his prayer about the publican. The Lord cannot bless such pathetic strategies of self-importance.

When I was in the seminary, a famous book about ministry told priests and other pastoral workers that we needed to pass from competition to compassion. As a seminarian, I did not understand how important the insight was. Pastoral ministry is, in fact, very susceptible to temptations of rivalry and competition. Pastoral workers are usually "people" people, by which I mean that they are naturally interested in the reactions of others and, inasmuch as they are sensitive to others, also very aware of how others relate to them. Thus, questions of popularity, of the response of the congregation or the students to one's best efforts, and all kinds of recognition issues are very important.

Sensitive people feel more for others and more because of others. A parish with several priests can sometimes reveal patterns of division that recall political constituencies. St. Paul talked about the problem with the Corinthians. Some had declared themselves for him, others for Apollos, others for Cephas, and still others for Christ (cf. 1 Corinthians 1:12). No one familiar with parochial life can miss our similarity with the Corinthians. The worst thing is when the ministers lend themselves to a kind of politics of division because of their need to feel needed. In fact, ministry is rife with competition, because the great temptation is to see the call in terms of self-validation and not in pure service. It is no wonder that the Lord told us what to say: "When you have done all that is commanded you, say, 'We are unworthy servants; we have only done what was our duty' " (Luke 17:10).

But this problem of competition is not just a problem of rectories, convents, and staff meetings. The spirit of rivalry lives in almost all hearts. Parents sometimes compete for the love of their children. The shtick of a comedy team of brothers when I was growing up had to do with one claiming at the slightest pretext, "Mom always liked you best." The humor was the inevitability of the comic's tracing all that was disagreeable to the lack of maternal justice. The disgrace of family life is the competition within the home. Original sin makes us want to justify ourselves at the expense of those close to us. Cain was upset that his sacrifice had not found favor with God, whatever that meant. His brother Abel became the victim of Cain's disappointed attempt at self-validation. The second sin in the history of humanity is not of pride but of envy.

The patience of Jesus is no more evident in the Scriptures than in his impromptu lesson after he asks this question. He has been telling them that he will suffer and they have refused to understand him. Nevertheless, he sits them down and he teaches them with infinite patience that they must serve one another. To underline the tenderness of the lesson, he shows them a child whom he enfolds in his arms. The image tells us more than the words. Love one another, the Master tells us. Forget about competition.

We live in an anxious, envious age. The insecurity of life is what pushes us at times to competition. It is as if we don't believe that there is enough love to go around, and so we have to fight for a better share. The false consolation of thinking that I am more important than another, or that my work is more valuable, or that I am luckier, or better liked, is a trap. Jesus says to us, "What were you talking about along the way?" (cf. Mark 9:33) — even though the dialog sometimes took place only in our hearts.

Were you thinking that you are better or more important than another person? Put yourselves in the arms of Jesus. The only answer to our insecurity and our need for power or attention is to convince ourselves of the love of God for us. ◇

"Salt is good; but if the salt has lost its saltness, how will you season it?" — Mark 9:50

First of all, we need to remember that Jesus was not talking chemistry here. There is no question of NaCl (sodium chloride) becoming something else. The use of the word "salt" is figurative. In fact, we could say that this saying and question of Jesus is a mini-parable. It is a short story that asks us to imagine salt that has lost its saltness. In St. Matthew, this is told with even a tragic ending: The salt is thrown out and trampled by men (cf. Matthew 5:13), a touch that recalls for me some of the briefer tales of Hans Christian Andersen. The title would be "The Tragedy of the Salt That Lost Its Flavor."

Unfortunately, the story is not fantastical in the life of the Church. In fact, it is the sad history of many of us sometimes and some of us more frequently. For that reason we need to reflect on the fate of saltless salt.

There are two characteristics of salt that make it a good metaphor for discipleship. Salt was the first chemical preservative known to man. With that we have a note of perseverance in the faith. Immediately after this question, Jesus says, "Have salt in yourselves, and be at peace with one another" (Mark 9:50). The "salt" in question, he implies, conserves the bond of Christian charity between disciples.

Another characteristic of salt is that it permeates other substances and gives them taste. The poor here in El Salvador who have nothing to eat are reduced to eating tortillas with salt. They are thick tortillas, not like the Mexican ones, which are sometimes paper-thin. But without salt the thick tortillas would be very difficult to swallow, because they would have no taste.

We should keep in mind that this question comes in a session in which Jesus is teaching his disciples in the house at Capernaum. He is saying to them — and through them, to us — that the disciple must have perseverance, and that perseverance is connected to mission. "Keep the faith," he is saying, and at the same time, "Keep spreading it around."

The two ideas are intrinsically related, and perhaps thinking of our example to others can help us to live the Christian life more intensely. The great French writer François Mauriac once wrote, "If our hearts do not burn with the love of Christ, there are others who will die from the cold."

Do you feel responsible for the faith of others? I think most of us secretly resent such a thought. We are the products of a society that prizes individualism as one of the greatest of qualities. There is something in our heads that says "yes" to "Row your own boat!" "You made the bed, now sleep in it." "You go your way, and I'll go mine." There is something very American about "Don't blame *me*," even though our courts are swamps of litigation seeking financial compensation for damages.

When we say of someone that he or she is "the salt of the earth," we generally refer to the fact that we can count on that person to be good. Sometimes we think that this is a question of nature, that some persons are congenitally altruistic or giving to others. I doubt that this is the case. It seems to me that some people are more practiced in self-sacrifice.

Are we in danger of being salt without flavor? Do we take every opportunity to make our position clear to others? Is your faith the most salient characteristic about you for others? Are there people in your life who do not even know about your connection to the Church? Has the ideal of not judging others and toleration of opinions become a sort of indifference to the truth of our religion? Do we say, "It works for me," painting our belief as a personal taste if not an innocent foible, like a delight in stories with happy endings or a sentimental tenderness for animals?

I am not talking about aggressive attitudes or judgmental postures. The English writer Rebecca West said it very well: "The point is that nobody likes having salt rubbed into their wounds, even if it is the salt of the earth." The poet Yeats, in his beautiful poem "A Prayer for My Daughter," wrote a very wise observation. Reflecting on a former friend whom he called "the loveliest woman born," who had practically become "an old bellows full of angry wind," he prays that his daughter's mind not "be choked with hate," which is "of all evil chances chief."

Giving testimony of faith does not mean hate. It means a passionate identification with Jesus, a living grafted onto him, a communion with his love that can never *not* be expressed. In fact, this identification-in-love might mean that others reject us or even hate us. That means that Yeats's "assault and battery of mind" cannot take away from us the basic joy of a believer. Serenity is a sign of faith and an acceptance of an identity.

Obviously, this question makes us reflect upon our Christian identity. Salt cannot be anything but salt. "The Tragedy of the Salt That Lost Its Flavor" might have the salt attempting to be something it could not be, like sugar. Then it could be discovered that precisely what was needed was salt. But the salt would have lost its "saltness" without taking on any other quality, like sweetness. Thus it would serve for nothing.

So too, the Christian who has lost his or her "salt." In the days of the Roman legion, salt was so valuable that the legionaries were paid in blocks of it. It is assumed that therein is the source of the expression "worth his salt." The soldier was worth his pay. I think that we might say of a Christian, is his or her "salt" worth it? Is mine? Is yours? ◇

"What did Moses command you?" — Mark 10:3

Jesus is typically responding to a question with a question here. Some Pharisees have come up to him "in order to test him" (Mark 10:2). They have asked him about whether it is lawful for a man to divorce his wife. Scholars have speculated about what the Pharisees were hoping for by asking him about divorce.

The subject was a matter of controversy for the rabbis. We are told in the Old Testament that a man who marries a woman who then "finds no favor in his eyes because he has found some indecency in her" (Deuteronomy 24:1) can write and give her a certificate of divorce and send her away. There were two schools about divorce. That of Shammai held that the only "indecency" that would justify divorce was infidelity. The school of Hillel gave "indecency" a broad interpretation. If a man did not like her cooking, her way of speaking, her attitude toward his relatives, or even her looks, he was free to divorce the woman.

In either school, the woman was not free to divorce a man, nor to oppose the proceedings if her husband wanted to be rid of her. Divorce represented therefore the absolute power of the husband over the wife. He could send her home to her family. The law on divorce helps us to understand the position of women in ancient Israel. Jesus was asked to comment on their state indirectly when he was questioned about his ideas on divorce.

Had the Pharisees heard that Jesus was against divorce? Perhaps not, because the disciples ask Jesus about the teaching afterward when they are alone. There might have been an instinctive feeling, however, that Jesus would not be able to justify his position in terms of the Law of Moses.

Jesus immediately refers to Moses in his response. The Pharisees respond that "Moses allowed a man to write a certificate of divorce, and to put her away" (Mark 10:4). There is an implication in this that his questioners were on the more liberal side of the rabbinical debate. The Lord's response to them must have overwhelmed them, because he gave an interpretation of why Moses permitted divorce: It was because of "your hardness of heart" (Mark 10:5) that he gave such a commandment.

Some scholars see in this that Moses made the divorce formal to impel some respect for the divorced woman. At the time of Christ, the divorce papers were written up by rabbis and registered with the Sanhedrin. It meant that a man could not send his wife home one day and ask for her the next week. Her ability to enter into another marriage was also guaranteed by the writ of divorce.

Jesus may have been saying that Moses had made a bad thing more tolerable by giving a minimum of protection to the woman. The original law in Deuteronomy had already anticipated that a man might want to go back to a wife who was divorced by the second husband, and had prohibited such a marriage. The Lord goes much further than ruling out capricious decisions. He prohibits divorce entirely. He proclaims this as a return to the divine intention of marriage as expressed in the first book of the Bible: "Therefore a man leaves his father and his mother and cleaves to his wife, and they become one flesh" (Genesis 2:24).

It is not hard to see that Jesus' teaching was very favorable for women, who would not have the threat of divorce in the air every time dinner turned out badly. The teaching also shows how Jesus wants to recuperate the divine intention for marriage. The indissolubility of marriage is based on the fact that marriage is a covenant, not a contract. The Christian teaching is a restoration of the mystery of the love between man and woman that creates family.

All of this is in the background of this question. In the foreground, and probably most alarmingly for the Pharisees, is the authority Jesus assumes to criticize and even to correct the Law of Moses by interpreting the motivation of a commandment. According to the great Bible scholar Joachim Jeremias, one of the pillars of Jesus' teaching was that his message was grounded in the Jewish Scriptures, what we call the Old Testament. Nevertheless, within the continuity he preached, Jesus revealed a "new" relationship with God, a new covenant that went further than the old. This episode reveals one of the ways that the New Testament, or "Covenant" (the real sense of the word "Testament"), differed from the Old.

Perhaps for us this question of Jesus can help us to recognize two critical points of our faith: the continuity of the Old and New Testaments and the fact that all the Bible must be understood in terms of Jesus Christ. Again we see the importance of the insight of Hans Urs von Balthasar: "Scripture is the word of God that bears witness to God's Word." All that we consider the word of God has to be understood in terms of Jesus (the Word of God). We *should* know what Moses commanded, but we *need* to know what Jesus commanded. Our key to the Scriptures is Jesus.

Thus I can take this question on several levels. Do I know what the Old Testament says? Do I know how that might differ from what Jesus says? Finally, this requires that I orient myself by means of the Scriptures, that it be the crucial reference to all my ideas about conduct.

Have you opened up the Old Testament? Do you know what Moses commanded? Have you entered into a relationship with the word of God that makes this question very basic and logical? That relationship can only be nurtured by study and commitment to learn. ◇

"Why do you call me good?" — Mark 10:18

This is certainly one of the most puzzling statements of Jesus in the Gospels because someone could take it to imply that he is denying his own goodness. The Fathers of the Church worried about this, as can be seen in the *Catena Aurea*. St. John Chrysostom said that Jesus was answering the man who knelt before him as a man. St. Bede the Venerable pointed out that Jesus had spoken of himself as the "*Good* Shepherd," to indicate that the question was not a denial of goodness nor divinity. Another ancient source thought that Jesus was hinting at his divinity to the man. "You don't know how right you are to call me so," is the implied message.

A modern commentator, William Barclay, echoed one of the Fathers by saying that Jesus was rejecting the man's supposed flattery. Mark 10:17 has the man, whom I always imagine to be a bit out of breath because he runs to stop Jesus and then genuflects before him, saying, "Good Teacher, what must I do to inherit eternal life?" Barclay says:

> Jesus did two things that every evangelist and every preacher and every teacher ought to remember and to copy. First he said in effect, "Stop and think! You are all wrought up and palpitating with emotion! I don't want you swept to me by a moment of emotion. Think calmly of what you are doing. . . ." Second, he said in effect, "You cannot become a Christian by a sentimental passion for me. You must look at God."
>
> —*Daily Study Bible for the New Testament:*
> *Gospel of Mark*, by William Barclay,
> Westminster John Knox Press, 1975

There is a hint of impetuousness in St. Mark's presentation of the man, whom St. Matthew also indicates as a young person. He is running to stop Jesus before Our Lord moves on and he asks him a question that implies a very profound answer. His sincerity apparently is without question, because we are told that Jesus "looking upon him loved him" (Mark 10:21). Just as quickly, Jesus' answer makes the man sad, and he continues on his way, going off even before Jesus does. He had been the person stopping Jesus from going on, remember?

Was he trying to flatter Jesus? I do not think it was as simple as that. If it were, it would be like that horrible grandmother in Flannery O'Connor's short story, "A Good Man Is Hard to Find," who keeps calling the homicidal maniac a "good man" because she hopes that he will spare her. She doesn't believe the man is good at all but wants him to think she does. This man really is anxious to hear what Jesus has to say. He is not setting up a trap, like some of Jesus' questioners, or if there is a trap, he falls in it himself. His sadness in walking away from the Lord reveals both his failure to embrace the evangelical life and, ironically, his confidence — or at least his fear — that Jesus is telling the truth. I think he does believe that Jesus is good, and his racing to speak with the Lord is a sign of his anxiety about his own goodness.

However, the man is doing something worse and more harmful than trying to flatter the Lord. He is expecting an easy message from him. We do the same thing when we pray for things without saying, "But let not my will but yours be done." Unfortunately, we do that all the time. This is shown when a trial comes into our life and we find it hard to reconcile with our belief in a good God. People lose faith and even become resentful with Jesus because of suffering. Unconsciously we do not want to be obedient to God. We want an obedient "god" of our own making.

We should never judge others, especially not when they have suffered more than we have. However, this question of

Jesus could be applied to us in this way. Jesus is saying, "When you come to me calling me good, which is calling me God, you really only want me to confirm your own wishes." We could often express the third petition of the Our Father more honestly by saying, "my will be done." If we approach the Lord in prayer we must be conscious of him as the only absolutely good thing. That should condition all our prayer.

The young and rich man had directed himself to Jesus, hoping perhaps for some sort of validation of his own spiritual life. He thought that he was doing well but wanted to make sure that he was doing all that he really needed. Maybe he had heard of the baptism of John and wondered if that was required, or whether Jesus had some new precept for the people. Instead, Jesus invites him to discipleship, a very frightening discipleship that includes ridding himself of his many possessions and living insecurely with the wandering Master.

Instead of a contract, he is offered a covenant. He had hoped to fill certain requirements and be secure in salvation. Jesus indicates to him the way of the cross, the scary freedom of the loss of self in the will of the Father. He rejects the opportunity to follow Jesus for his possessions. Did he live to regret his decision? Did he get a second chance to follow Jesus? I try to imagine the life of the young man as he grew older and wonder whether he died a rich man.

I suppose I should be more concerned about myself, however. Why do I call Jesus good? Do I approach him hoping for the easy answer? Am I ready to accept his call? What about you? ◇

And he said to them, "What do you want me to do for you?"
— Mark 10:36

James and John have come up to the Lord and exclaimed, "Teacher, we want you to do for us whatever we ask of you" (Mark 10:35). The abruptness of this is startling in context, but we can imagine that the two brothers had been discussing the proposal for some time privately. In fact, St. Matthew, in chapter 20, verses 20-23, has the mother of James and John ask Jesus the favor (if you can call something so overreaching as sitting at the right and left of Jesus in heaven a "favor"), making the ambition all in the family. However, it is noteworthy that Jesus does not respond to the wife of Zebedee in St. Matthew but directs his response to her sons.

In both Gospels, the petition for power comes right after Jesus has predicted his Passion and death. Cheek by jowl with the annunciation of suffering and death, the request appears in all its absurdity. The disciples were interested in the glory of an earthly kingdom, and Jesus was about to die as a common criminal. The train was rolling to a stop when they were fighting for good seats.

The irony is lost on the disciples, however, who proceed to make their request. What was Jesus thinking? The Bible tells us that Jesus could read the hearts of men, so I do not doubt that he knew what the disciples were going to say. As we have seen, this was not the first time that ambition had reared its ugly head among the twelve apostles. What patience the Lord had with his disciples! We use the expression "Three times and you are out." Christ obviously did not feel the same way. In fact, this question appears in the third part of a triple teaching about suffering and death. Each time Jesus teaches about the fact that he must suffer, the disciples respond inappropriately. The first time Peter rebukes the Lord (cf. Mark 8:32); the second time the disciples get into an argument along the way to Capernaum (cf. Mark 9:34); and the third time (this reading) James and John decide to pop their question to Jesus.

My own reaction to this question of Jesus is to realize that my own relationship to the Lord can verge on the model presented by the two apostles. "We want you to do whatever we ask of you," they say as a preface to this question (cf. Mark 10:36). How often our prayer lives could be summed up in the same pathetic way!

I remember an incident in the seminary that makes a good cross-reference. Most of the seminarians were nervous about preaching to their peers. The nerves often resulted in bloopers, which often resulted in jokes for days. One of the more stuffy of the deacon class was preaching one day on the sixth chapter of Isaiah. He suggested that we take the same attitude as the prophet in fulfilling the mission of Jesus to evangelize. Isaiah 6:8 reads verbatim: "Then I said, 'Here am I! Send me.' " My friend the deacon wound up to a kind of rhetorical height and said, "Here am I, *serve* me." Some of the brethren started laughing and I was one of them, I must confess.

One of the few things I accept from Freud are that slips of the tongue are sometimes very revealing. The preacher's slip of the tongue might have been a good one for any one of us. Our attitude in prayer is sometimes, "My will be done." We approach Jesus and think that what we ask of him is necessary in some ultimate way.

An old lady in my congregation once asked me to keep an intention of hers in mind for the next week. Then the next week, and the one after that, and she always asked me whether I was truly praying for her petition. I learned after about a month that the woman was expecting to win the lottery. She had promised God that the Church would get the money, and so she expected that she had to win. Apparently, she had thought it an offer that God could not refuse. When I teased her about her attitude, she said that God was being unreasonable. "My thoughts are not your thoughts . . . , says the LORD," I told her, quoting Isaiah 55:8. Nevertheless, I know that I have sometimes identified my approach to a problem or my prayer for a solution as the only way. Just like the apostles, I am ready to rush in with my request.

Sometimes even our prayer is selfish, and that is the lesson we can get to by following this question of Jesus through to its intention. Often our prayer is noble, but many times it is self-centered. Ultimately prayer is in our own best interest, but it should not be self-interested. It is necessary to examine our prayer for selfishness at times, to purify it and make it a communion with God's will and not lobbying for a wish list.

We should pray for more strength, not for lighter crosses. And our perspective always has to be otherworldly. Material things have to be seen as secondary. There is a Latin expression, *sub specie aeternitatis*, "under the aspect of eternity." Our prayer should always include an awareness that we are pilgrims on this earth and that our projects are trivial compared with the great plan of God. Milton expressed this when he has Patience say in his sonnet on blindness: "God doth not need / Either man's works or his own gifts. Who best / Bear his mild yoke, they serve him best; his state / Is kingly; thousands at his bidding speed, / And post o'er land and ocean without rest; / They also serve who only stand and wait."

But what do you think? Imagine that you have some particular petition about your life, your job, some relationship. You look into the eyes of Jesus, and he asks you this question. What happens? ◇

"Are you able to drink the cup that I drink, or to be baptized with the baptism with which I am baptized?" — Mark 10:38

Sometimes I think of this question of Jesus at the Eucharist and it makes me feel a bit uncomfortable. What can I say to Jesus? Do I honestly respond, "Who, me? I am afraid to say that I don't know." If I said, "Yes, I am able," I would be lying.

What is the cup that Jesus had to drink? William Barclay tells us that "cup" in biblical language represented the experience of life. For that reason the psalmist, grateful to God, says that his cup overflows (cf. Psalm 23:5). But the cup could also be symbolic of bitter experience. The prophet Isaiah talks about the cup of God's wrath (cf. Isaiah 51:17). It is in this sense of cup that Jesus prays in the agony in the garden, "Abba, Father, all things are possible to thee; remove this cup from me; yet not what I will, but what thou wilt"(Mark 14:36).

John and James were seeking the glory of sitting at the right hand and the left hand of Jesus in the kingdom. Their mistake is obvious to us who know about the Passion and death that Jesus was about to suffer. St. John Chrysostom, in the *Catena Aurea*, translates this question of Jesus to the ambitious apostles in this way: "You speak of honors, but I am discoursing of wrestlings and toil; for this is not a time of rewards, but of blood, battles, and dangers."

Reverend Martin Luther King, Jr., who was the winner of the Nobel Peace Prize in 1964, commented upon the ambition of James and John and spoke of the "drum major instinct." Dr. King saw the instinct as good because it gives good fruit. Where would the Church be if some did not want to be in leadership positions? The ambition to serve was good, but it had to be purified, said Dr. King in a sermon. The purification was the participation in the suffering of the Lord. You had to know what you were asking for when you desired to lead in the Church.

Nevertheless, this seems to be playing a little too close to what T. S. Eliot described as "the greatest treason: / to do the right deed for the wrong reason" *(Murder in the Cathedral)*. St. Paul, in 1 Corinthians 13:1-3, describes all the prodigies that can be done but which are worth nothing if love is not their motive. In fact, Jesus' question here is an admitted *non sequitur*. He says that regardless of their drinking the cup and enduring the baptism, the seats at his right and left are not his to give. Jesus has taken the pretext of their ambition in order to say something to them about the reality of suffering in the kingdom.

He is talking about himself, pointing out that he absorbed the poison of sin in order to save us. In El Salvador, there are still stories of poisonous snakes. A man I know was saved when bitten by a venomous snake because his father sucked the poison from the wound just like we have seen in Westerns. What if the poison was so great that the one who saved the other would have to die? That is the cup of suffering that Jesus accepted.

What about his baptism? Baptism comes from the word in Greek "to submerge" and we must understand that Jesus is talking here about a submersion in an experience that is all-inclusive — that is why it is symbolized by going underwater. He plunged into the cesspool of human experience; he was completely immersed within it. St. Paul tells us that Jesus was made sin for us (cf. 2 Corinthians 5:21), and it is important that we remember the implied distinction: made not a *sinner* but *sin itself*. Our Lord took upon himself the ugliness of the world, the bitterness of its constant history of treason, the awful odor of rotting flesh opposing the will of God. The French poet Paul Claudel has the story in one of his plays of a young and beautiful virgin who kisses a leper to cure him of his disease. He is cured; she contracts the disease and is left alone. Our salvation was much like that kiss of a leper.

What could be the equivalent of the kiss of the leper in our lives? Recently a friend told me about a woman who had been abandoned by her husband. In desperation she left her country to live with some of her children in *el Norte* ("the North"), as people here talk about the United States. Her life was stable and presumably she was doing well. Then her unfaithful husband had a stroke. The family had a conference about what should be done and the wife decided to be the caregiver. For her, this was a simple case of "for better or worse, in sickness and in health." While I would never advise someone like her that she was obliged to do something like that, I can only admire the woman.

I suppose that she never stopped loving the man. She is also very conscious about how her children were worried about their father. For her, the vows of matrimony represent a commitment that is unconditional, something that is rare in these days. Without a doubt, there are some who would say that she should not make herself responsible for someone who had shown himself untrue. If this is not an example of redeeming love, I do not know what is. Bedridden, incontinent, and at times incoherent, her husband represents a cross almost absurdly heavy. Talk about drinking the cup of suffering or being baptized by fire! It is common these days to hear self-sacrificing people called all sort of names, including some that reveal more pretension than knowledge of psychology. While there is a difference between the victimhood of Christ and victimization, it is also true that our age does not have a lot of sympathy for the idea of sacrifice.

Probably no age ever did, really, but sometimes in the past there was more of a disguising of self-interest. Chrysostom's words for discipleship are very striking: "wrestlings and toil," "blood, battles, and dangers." Are we really ready for all that? I wonder how many of us Christians really are prepared to give the submission to God's will that faith demands. Dietrich Bonhoeffer talked about "the cost of discipleship" and about people who wanted "cheap grace." He should be living at this hour, since the Church has need of him, to paraphrase Wordsworth.

How would I answer this question of the Lord? Herman Melville has a classic short story about a man who works in a lawyer's office in nineteenth-century New York City. He is a strange type, and his employer is maddened by what is a constant refrain in Bartleby's conversation, "I would prefer not to." I suppose I would like to pull a Bartleby the Scrivener on this question and prefer not even to think about the cost of discipleship in my own life.

Unfortunately, this question of Jesus is inescapable for the Christian. We are all to drink of the Messiah's cup and be baptized in his baptism. Inevitably, the life of a Christian has to become an "imitation of Christ." That means union to his saving love. That means the experience of the cross. Really this question is another way of asking, "Can you take up your cross and follow me?"

How do you answer it? ◇

150

"What do you want me to do for you?"   — Mark 10:51

When I first started reflecting about this question of Jesus, I thought that we would all like to have a chance to hear Jesus say, "What do you want me to do for you?" However, as I meditated a bit, I wondered what I would say to a question so open. I decided that the blind man had it easier than us. He obviously would improve his life if he had sight. But if you don't have a similar impediment, what do you ask for? Certainly you would not want to waste a chance like this question on what I call an Aladdin's lamp gambit, asking for some material thing with no future.

A friend of mine in the seminary stopped to give a ride to a man on a cold day. Despite the freezing temperatures, the man was not dressed for the outside. My friend has a warm heart and picked up the stranger, opening the door of his old Volkswagen bug and welcoming the man in. The man settled in and my friend very affably asked him, "Where are you going, brother?"

The answer was somewhat unexpected. The man started shouting at him: "How am I supposed to know where I am going? I have nowhere to go! You think that I have a place to go? I have no place!"

It turned out the man was homeless, one of many of the same with some kind of psychological disorder. He was, to the consternation of the Good Samaritan who picked him up, quite simply not rational. My friend lost a day trying to take him to centers and realizing how difficult it is to place someone who is not reasonable but does not want psychiatric treatment. The seminarian was shaken by the experience and recounted the story many times. What caught my attention, and makes me remember the incident, is the question "How am I supposed to know where I am going?"

Irresistibly, I think someone might want to respond to Jesus, "How am I supposed to know what I want?" There are those who do not have enough faith to ask for more of it. There are others spiritual enough to believe Jesus will give them what they need and materialistic enough to think that what they want is what they need. Remember the little old lady I told you about who was quite upset that God had not let her win the lottery when it was clear that that was the best solution all around?

But for people who have known the Lord for a while, it is not so easy to think about what we should ask of Jesus. I think that Bartimaeus really has given us the best answer: "Master, that I may see," which is a more literal translation of the Greek. This miracle of giving sight is the second one in St. Mark. The repetition alerts us to the symbolic importance of the healing, as does the conclusion of the incident. Jesus found himself facing many who were blind to him and his message. The lack of faith was the essential lack of vision of the people. The dramatic circumstances of the giving of sight to this particular blind man help us to see the symbolic importance.

Jesus is on the road to Jerusalem when Bartimaeus greets him, calling him by the messianic title, "Son of David." The blind man has "seen" that Jesus is the Messiah. By his recognition of Jesus, he anticipates the Lord's triumphal entry into Jerusalem that will follow (and which he himself probably saw when it took place). The others in the crowd anticipate another reaction when they tell Bartimaeus that he should desist from shouting to Jesus. Paradoxically, they are blind while he can see.

There is an interesting detail to the miracle. Jesus says, "Go your way" (Mark 10:52), to the man even before he has received his sight. In other miracles in the New Testament, Jesus says the same thing — for example, when he tells the centurion in Matthew 8:13 that he may go home because his servant has been healed. Here it makes a claim on our attention because only after hearing the words does the man recover his power to see. Ironically, he disobeys the literal meaning of Jesus' expression and begins to follow Jesus on the road to Jerusalem.

This conclusion gives a clue about the mystical meaning of the passage. The man decides in a flash to become a follower of Jesus. His second sight had given him the courage to call upon Jesus as the Son of David. His physical sight enables him to follow him. What did he see in the next few days of the Passion and death of the Lord? Did he become afraid, along with the other, more veteran disciples? I think that whatever happened, he was to become a part of the early Christian community in post-Paschal Jerusalem. If he did not, how could it be that St. Mark would remember his name? I even imagine Bartimaeus as an old man recounting his "love at first sight" that changed his life completely.

There was a game show on television for years in which contestants often congratulated each other with the expression "good answer" in their competition. Bartimaeus certainly deserved that praise in his answer to Christ's question. That takes me back to the idea of how we might answer the same.

St. Richard of Chichester was a bishop in twelfth-century England. He is famous for composing a prayer that has been prayed by generations and even made into a song in *Godspell*: "Day by day, dear Lord, help me to see Thee more clearly, love Thee more dearly, and follow Thee more nearly." The classic triad of knowing, loving, and serving would make a good answer with which we might respond to this question of Jesus.

"What do I want from you, Lord? Like the blind Bartimaeus, I would like to see you. Seeing you would make me love you, I know, because you are all good. Loving you would inspire me to serve you. Lord, that I would see!" ◇

"Is it not written, 'My house shall be called a house of prayer for all the nations'?" — Mark 11:17

The scene for this question is the dramatic cleansing of the forecourt of the Temple. It helps in this regard to remember that animal sacrifice was the principal liturgy of the Jewish Temple. Essentially, there was a market within the Temple, administered by the priests, to make it easier for the pious, offering sacrifice, to purchase the required animal or bird. Pilgrims who wanted to offer sacrifice often could not bring an animal from their home, and, if they did, it had to be approved for sacrifice by the priests. Animals purchased in the Temple must have been preapproved. It was certainly more convenient to buy the victim for sacrifice in the market in the Court of the Gentiles.

More convenient but not cheaper. Convenience had its price in New Testament times as it does today — surely anyone who has bought a sandwich in an airport would agree. William Barclay mentions that in the Talmud it is reported that when Rabbi Simon ben Gamaliel heard of the high price of a pair of doves for sacrifice he insisted that the price be lowered from one gold piece to a silver one. What was true of the booths selling animals was also true of the moneychangers, who imposed a surcharge on changing Roman and Greek coins to those minted for the Temple. Since the Temple tax had to be paid in the Temple's own coin, the administration gained twice: on the change and on the tax.

It is consoling to think that the heart of Jesus was stirred to anger at these unjust business practices because it means that he was concerned for those most affected, the poor. Anyone who has had the grace of working with the poor has to feel strengthened by this aspect of the cleansing of the Temple. Could Jesus see the poor people lined up to buy a pair of turtle-doves at inflated prices and not think of his own mother and foster father who had made a similar sacrifice when he was born? He had been moved by the widow who gave her mite to the Temple treasury. How could he not resent the corruption of excessive charges for sacrifices required by the law? No wonder that he remembered Jeremiah 7:11, which talked about making the Temple a robbers' den.

But the economic issue was not the only one that Jesus was concerned about. The German Bible scholar Ulrich Wilcken has pointed out that the animal market was in the only part of the Temple in which Gentiles were permitted entry. There was even a sign on the door to the next court saying that non-Jews would be executed for moving closer to the sanctuary. It is significant that Jesus quotes Isaiah 56:7, because it an expression of the universalist current in the Old Testament, one that saw a time ahead when all the nations would worship the true God together. The Court of the Gentiles, with its prohibition of further entry into the place consecrated with God's presence, was a contradiction to Isaiah's prophecy.

Jesus saw himself as the new Temple of Presence. For that reason he made reference to the destruction of the Temple and its being raised up in three days. The Jews believed that God lent his *Shekinah*, his special presence, to the Temple. The rabbis, commenting on the destruction of Solomon's Temple by the Babylonians, talked about a vision of the *Shekinah* as some kind of supernatural and feminine form that walked mournfully out of the Holy City.

In Jesus we meet more than a special presence of God. He is God the Son, who became one *of* us to become one *with* us. He is our access to the Divine, just as the Temple in Jerusalem was once a unique place of encounter with God. Mixing metaphors, which the Bible likes to do sometimes, we can see ourselves as the living stones of the new and spiritual temple of God's presence. Through Jesus Christ, according to 1 Peter 2:4-5, we become both a new temple and a new priesthood to facilitate the encounter between God and man.

I see that there are two applications that we can make about this question of Jesus. First of all, there is the sense of meeting the Lord and a recognition of his place in our life because of an actual place. Jesus was incensed that the Temple, which was dedicated to his Father, was debased by greed and obstruction, if not opposition, to God's universal love. Our own church, the churches we visit, should be places of prayer for us. We should sense when we are on the hallowed ground of encounter with the Lord, especially when the prayers of others have made holy a particular place.

Second, we should have a sense of our own vocation to be "living stones . . . built into a spiritual house," as St. Peter tells us in 1 Peter 2:5. That means we should be signs of God's presence and facilitators of encounter with him. Our own prayer life is a guarantee that we can be a sign of God's presence to his people. We need to be spiritual people despite the army of distractions that lays siege to us and despite the desires of the flesh that war against the soul (cf. 1 Peter 2:11).

God's presence is solidarity. That is why the rejection of injustice is so crucial for Christians. Jesus resented the exploitation of the poor in the buying and selling in the Temple, which made it a robbers' den. Both individually and collectively we have to free ourselves of sins against solidarity. The universal love that the prophet Isaiah preached requires as a minimum a refusal to seek material advantage of others. Citizens of the richest and most powerful country on earth, we need to be worried about this much more than we are. The market in the Temple showed how corruption could coexist in physical proximity to works of piety. Unfortunately the two can coexist in our own souls as well. ◇

"Was the baptism of John from heaven or from men?"

— Mark 11:30

The chief priests and the scribes and the elders had found him in the Temple and asked "by what authority" he was "doing these things," as pointed out in Mark 11:27-28. They are still angry about the cleansing of the Temple and fearful about the way the multitude listens to Jesus. Their question is not what we could call a point of information. Rather it is a challenge to Jesus' authority, basically as rhetorical a question as when we say to someone, "With what right are you doing this?" The implication is that Jesus has no authority. From whom could he receive it if not from the very questioners, the religious establishment of the Judaism at the time?

Jesus refuses to answer the question of the chief priests and their company if they do not declare themselves on the subject of John the Baptist. This is a very clever strategy, because it confronts the leadership with a dilemma. Do they lose face before the people, who instinctively recognized the Baptist as a prophet, or do they pretend to accept the teaching of a man they had detested? St. Mark tells of their consultation between themselves and their "safe" conclusion, "We do not know" (Mark 11:33).

Their question pretended to ask what they already knew; their feigned ignorance pretended that they did not have an established opinion about John. Jesus does not accept that they do not know about John. He takes their false humility as the refusal to answer that it is and so says, "Neither will I tell you by what authority I do these things" (Mark 11:33).

But his question was not just a clever dodging of a question. It is clear that the ministry of John the Baptist contained the answer to the priests' question. The baptism of John was crucial to the mission of Jesus, as the New Testament makes very clear. The preparation for the Redeemer that was John's vocation was most definitely "from God." Those who recognized the baptism of John would recognize that Jesus was the promised Messiah and therefore his authority also came "from God."

The Swiss theologian Hans Urs von Balthasar worried about the lack of theological reflection in our day about John the Baptist, who is so important in the Gospels. The scholar felt that the tendency to ignore the Baptist diminished our understanding of Jesus. If he was not irrelevant in the New Testament, why is he seemingly so in our own ideas?

John the Baptist came from the same priestly background as those who were questioning Jesus. From an early age, says St. Luke, he was called to the wilderness to preach the message of an impending end to existing order, "the wrath to come" (Luke 3:7), as John exclaimed to the crowds who came for baptism. Those who repented and received his baptism as a sign of their conversion would survive the baptism of fire to come.

A comparison with the ministry of Jesus makes for a series of contrasts. John was from the priestly caste, while Jesus was a "son" of David, of the tribe of Judah. John lived apart in the strictest kind of asceticism, dressing in the skin of animals and sustaining himself on locusts and wild honey; Jesus, on the other hand, ate and drank and was familiar with banquets, something we know both from his examples in teaching and from the number of times it is mentioned that he ate at grand houses. John stayed in the wilderness and there the people sought him out; Jesus went to the towns to preach the Good News. No miracles are reported of John; Jesus' ministry was sometimes so full of miracles that there was a danger that people only sought "signs" and would not listen to him. John directly confronted a personal moral failure of Herod the Tetrarch and for this was imprisoned and eventually executed; Jesus was falsely accused of political ambition and executed as an enemy of Tiberius Caesar, with a sign over his head that read, "Jesus of Nazareth, King of the Jews."

Despite these contrasts, the Baptist recognized Jesus as the Christ. His insight at the baptism of Jesus was confirmed by the title by which he called the Savior: "the Lamb of God" (John 1:29, 36). With Jesus, he was prophesying that there would be a new Passover. The blood of the new Lamb of Sacrifice would again deliver God's people. I think that some of the imagery of the Apocalypse (the book of Revelation) comes from an elaboration of the Baptist's intuition that Jesus was the Paschal Victim of a totally new order. The triumphant lamb on the throne in heaven was the same one whom John had pointed out on the riverbank (cf. John 1:36).

There is an essential mystery about the Baptist and his community of disciples, which eventually had offshoots even outside of Palestine (cf. Acts 19). Some scholars have associated him with the Essenes, who also had a kind of baptism (although this was self-administered and repeated). Others have vehemently denied any connection other than the fact that both he and the Essenes were part of the same panorama of religious ideas and experience that was the Judaism of their time. What is hard to tell is what gave this harsh preacher such a hold on the imagination of the people of his time and why Jesus was so impressed with him. Remember Jesus' enigmatic words about John, "I tell you, among those born of women none is greater than John; yet he who is least in the kingdom of God is greater than he" (Luke 7:28; cf. Matthew 11:11)?

It is easy for us to answer this question of Jesus with a facile and kind of automatic "from God." However, have we really understood what the Baptist taught us? Do we see his baptism as something that teaches us about the mystery of our salvation? In prayer and meditation, we ought to go out to the wilderness to be with one who is called the Precursor. The more we meditate on his ministry, the better we understand that of Jesus our Redeemer. ◇

"What will the owner of the vineyard do?"   — Mark 12:9

Usually the readers of an author ask what happens after the story. For that reason, there are sequels. But here we have a storyteller who asks his listeners for the conclusion of the story. I read somewhere about an author who was asked about the future of one of his fictitious characters. He said, "I didn't know what would happen next to her, and so I wrote another novel to find out." Jesus did not apparently have such doubts. His story of the vineyard was not meant to end in an ambiguity that would permit anyone to supply his or her own conclusion, like some modern works of literature. What would come after was obvious to him.

Parables are relatively very short stories and have stimulated some authors to imagine details that Jesus did not bother to include. André Gide, a Nobel Laureate in Literature, once wrote a story about the Prodigal Son, which includes the Prodigal's mother, as well as a younger brother who is also more than a little restless to see the world. We don't need to write a longer work based on the story of the vineyard, but we ought to look closely at some of its details. Familiarity with Scripture stories does not breed contempt but sometimes a kind of casual, inattentive reading.

The parable that inspires this question is amazing for the breadth of its subject in relation to the few words it contains. It is no less than a summary of salvation history from Creation to Calvary. The planting of the vineyard recalls Genesis 2:8, "And the LORD God planted a garden in Eden, in the east; and there he put the man whom he had formed." The man's job was "to till it and keep it" (Genesis 2:15). It is clear in both instances that the place is not given outright, that it does not belong to the man.

Then comes the harvest. The owner of the vineyard expects his share of what has been produced. This demand is as minimal as the command not to eat of a certain tree. But the first messenger is beaten and sent back empty-handed. Then the second is "struck on the head and insulted" says the literal Greek. A third is killed. After him, there are many others, each receiving abusive treatment. Obviously, these messengers represent the prophets of Israel who encountered resistance at almost every turn.

Finally, as we are told in Mark 12:6, he had "one other," the last messenger, the last recourse. Jesus was our last chance and, according to this story, God's last resort for reconciliation. I say reconciliation and not collection, which is the supposed original reason for the sending of the messengers, because the owner suddenly appears as a loving father, who expects the farmers to "respect my son." This makes it seem that more is at stake here than collecting the rent.

But, of course, they do not respect the son. They see in his coming the opportunity of taking over the vineyard definitively. This implies, of course, that this is the father's only son. With the heir out of the way, they will have no rival claims. There is certainly a resemblance here with, "You shall be like gods," the temptation that Satan dangles in front of Eve (cf. Genesis 3:5). "You will be your own authority. This land will be yours." The killing of the son and the maltreatment of his body represent a kind of definitive sin to be put alongside the original one.

The Resurrection is not included in this parable. It stops at the point before the burial, practically speaking, when the body is thrown outside the vineyard. At this critical point, Jesus stops the narrative and demands a response. What will happen next? Do you think that they will "get away with it," as we say in idiomatic English?

Some scholars of the Bible think that this parable is about the destruction of Jerusalem, which the early Christians saw as divine judgment for the enormous evil of putting God's Son to death. Certainly Jesus suggests in his own answer to his question that the vineyard was Israel. "He will come and destroy the tenants, and give the vineyard to others"(Mark 12:9). As in the parable of the wedding banquet in Matthew 22, there is a displacement implied and a replacement. Others will replace the first tenants, just as the banquet will now be offered to those from the hedgerows and byways.

But it is always dangerous to see the words of Christ as applicable only to others. We have our share in the guilt that the Lamb of God takes away. The question of the justice of God is always applicable to everyone. Although we do not believe in a God who punishes, we do believe that there are consequences connected with our conduct. It is not possible to reject the Son of God, thus repeating in a personal form all the rejections of recognizing God's power that have been made throughout history, without guaranteeing self-destruction. The all-powerful God takes us so seriously that he will not save us without our consent. He granted liberty to the tenants, although that meant his own Son had to be sacrificed.

There are many people today, even people we call "religious," who no longer believe in judgment. If movies and popular culture are any index of ideas of the afterlife, it appears that Americans believe in life after death but not in damnation. Some want a "no-fault" eternity, which will prolong our existence but not involve anything complicated like hell.

Nevertheless, the reality of judgment is integral to the history of salvation. That is how I take this question of Jesus. Do we believe that the acceptance of Jesus as Lord is crucial, essential, and absolutely necessary? Are we tempted to think sometimes that our faith is a matter of indifference? That there is no risk of destruction? Do we recognize that the history of salvation is one of decision? Not only should we think about our own decision but also about how we have helped others to decide.

One day we will know experientially what the owner of the vineyard will do. In faith we know already. We need to learn to live in accord with knowing the answer to this question of Our Lord. ◇

"Have you not read this scripture: / 'The very stone which the builders rejected / has become the head of the corner; / this was the Lord's doing, / and it is marvelous in our eyes'?"
— Mark 12:10-11

The Spanish Cardinal Rafael Merry del Val was the child of a Spanish diplomat and a lady of the English nobility. His father was the Spanish ambassador to the Vatican, and that probably helped his ecclesiastical career. At the age of thirty-five he was made an archbishop and then three years later a cardinal. He served as the Secretary of State for the Vatican while the saintly Pius X was pope.

But perhaps the servant was not as saintly as the pope, at least in certain things. One of Merry del Val's deputies in his secretariat was a certain Giacomo (Joachim) della Chiesa. After four years of working in the same secretariat, Della Chiesa was made an archbishop by Pius X and sent to Bologna. He was farmed out, so to speak, after having worked his whole priesthood in diplomatic assignments, and had to take up tasks that he had never done before, like visiting parishes.

At regular intervals, the pope names cardinals from the ranks of bishops who work in close collaboration with him or who have important dioceses. Twice Pius X decided to name Della Chiesa cardinal. Twice Merry del Val found pretexts for delaying the official announcement until too late. The third time the pope directly intervened so that Della Chiesa was made a cardinal in May of 1914, thus frustrating his own Secretary of State.

In August of 1914, the pope died. The cardinals were convoked for a conclave and in September elected Della Chiesa as Pope Benedict XV. As is still customary, the election was followed by a rite at which each cardinal kneels before the pope to signify his allegiance. Benedict XV seems to have relished it a bit when his archrival came to give his obeisance. "The stone which the builder rejected has become the cornerstone," said the new pope.

"It is the Lord who has done this work, and it is marvelous in our eyes," replied Merry del Val. Within a month he was no longer Secretary of State, although he continued working at the Vatican eight years after Benedict had died. He never regained his former authority, however, and it is interesting that the cleric who was the scourge of the modernists is now best remembered for a pious prayer called "The Litany of Humility."

Stories of rejection followed by success appeal to something deep within us. I think that is because the Lord has built into us a certain structure that enables us to recognize the truth. Whether this is in a trivial or comic form like in the song "Rudolph the Red-nosed Reindeer," and the fairy tale about the ugly duckling, or in the most important happening in the history of the universe, the Resurrection of Jesus, something in our spirit says, "Yes, that is what should happen." Would that all the ones who did the rejecting would have the grace of a Merry del Val to recognize in such moments a reflection of the glory of God.

Scholars are not sure of the original use of Psalm 118, the twenty-second verse of which Jesus quotes in Matthew 21:42, and which Pope Benedict XV and Cardinal Merry del Val also quoted. It was apparently connected to some sort of thanksgiving liturgy in the Temple in Jerusalem. The person (or is it a personified Israel?) expressing his gratitude to God had apparently been on the margin and then, to the surprise of opponents, had become the key person in what sounds like a victory in battle. The Spanish Bible scholar Luis Alonso Schokel has worked out a dramatic reading of the text, in which he sees some verses as a response to a soloist taking the part of the marginated-one-turned-savior. "A change so radical and unexpected," says Schokel, "appears to us as a miracle."

The New Testament quotes this verse of the psalm in five separate passages as a prophecy fulfilled in the person of Jesus. It is a proverb but at the same time a kind of parable. In two quick lines one imagines a story like something out of Hans Christian Andersen. First, there is the rejection of a stone by the builders. Then, the thing is cast off as useless while the other building climbs in construction. Finally, the stone becomes the cornerstone of a new and greater edifice.

But we need to go beyond the story itself. It is really a vehicle for the expression of how Jesus sees himself. He lived the mystery of death and Resurrection before the events took place. Three times he predicts his rejection by the leaders of his people and his suffering and death in St. Mark as something foreordained. Redemption is a process that inescapably includes rejection and apparent failure.

That lesson is complementary to the story of the owner of the vineyard that we have seen in the question that immediately precedes this one (cf. Mark 12:1-10). The owner's son was bound to come, and they were determined to kill him and would receive their punishment. But that would not be the end. Not only would the vineyard be given to others but also the son would come back to life. Jesus mixes metaphors by concluding a parable about a vineyard with a proverb about construction, but the connection is the theme of rejection. The parable is the consequences for the rejecters; the proverb is the promise of the rejected.

If we were to frame this question for ourselves, it would have to be in terms of the rejected. We are followers of the one who was rejected, reviled, murdered. "The world hated me," said Jesus; "how can it not hate you, too?" (cf. John 15:18). Where we see rejection, therefore, there is a reflection of the mystery of redemption and its movement from death to life.

"Do you not know," says Jesus, "that the Scripture predicts rejection as an essential process?" (cf. Matthew 5:11-12, 10:38-39). The details of what this means for you or me might be very different, but the general truth should make us pay attention. Where is the rejection in our life? Where is the sign that we are followers of the king who wore a crown of thorns? If our life here were cushy, would we be able to enter into the spirit of the psalmist's proclamation: "This is the LORD's doing; / it is wonderful in our eyes" (Psalm 118:23)?

Stefan Zweig wrote that only those who knew life's lowest valleys could really know it well. For the Christian this could be translated that only those who know the dark valley of death can appreciate the good news of the Resurrection. If we were really in tune with this painful mystery, we would know true consolation. ◇

"Why put me to the test?" — Mark 12:15

Mary McCarthy, an American woman of letters in the twentieth century, once said of another writer, Lillian Hellman, "Every word she writes is a lie, including 'and' and 'the.' " Something similar could be said about the Pharisees and Herodians who provoke this question of Jesus.

Chapters 11 and 12 of St. Mark are a rogues' gallery of the opposition to Jesus. In a series of encounters and confrontations, his opponents meet with Jesus in the Temple. We have already seen how Jesus dealt with the delegation from the "chief priests and scribes." In this passage, the encounter is with "some Pharisees and Herodians." Next there will be a duel with "the Sadducees," a more friendly interview with "one of the scribes," and finally Jesus will address the crowd that hears his words "gladly."

The chief priests and scribes had been interested in the event they saw as a direct challenge of their authority by Jesus: the cleansing of the Temple. When they are checkmated in their questioning of the Lord, they send a group of Pharisees and Herodians to him. The mission is double in deceit. First of all, the men are working for the chief priests and scribes. Second, they are very interested in trapping Jesus themselves, but their pretense is that they sincerely want his teaching on a difficult point of controversy.

St. Mark had already established that the Herodians and Pharisees were enemies of Jesus. Their unholy alliance was reported in Mark 3:6, when they joined forces in order "to destroy" Jesus. The provocation that makes them conspire against Jesus is the fact that the Lord cured the man with the withered hand on the Sabbath. In Mark 8:15, we see that Jesus had warned his disciples in the boat on the Sea of Galilee, "Take heed, beware of the leaven of the Pharisees and the leaven of Herod."

The confused disciples began to recriminate about who forgot to buy the bread (cf. Mark 8:16), but New Testament readers cannot fail to remember that Jesus said that "the leaven" of the Pharisees was "hypocrisy" (Luke 12:1). Here, too, Jesus recognizes "their hypocrisy" (Mark 12:15).

The word hypocrisy comes from the Greek theater vocabulary and means "playing a part." When the Hebrew Bible was translated into the Greek of the Septuagint, the word for theatrical representation was used to describe the attitude of a person who did not obey God. Some scholars do not see any connection of the original sense of the Greek word with its use in the New Testament.

Nevertheless, the theatrical connection is appropriate in this case because there can be no doubt of the "performance" put on by the Pharisees and Herodians in posing their question to Jesus: "Teacher, we know that you are true, and care for no man; for you do not regard the position of men, but truly teach the way of God. Is it lawful to pay taxes to Caesar, or not?" (Mark 12:14). Analyzing the lies in this single sentence brought McCarthy's famous remark about Hellman to my mind. They did not really accept Jesus as *teacher*, nor did they think that he was *true*, nor did they really think that he had no regard for men, since they feared the crowd's sympathy for him, and finally, they did not think that he *truly taught* the way of God.

St. Mark does not say whether anyone was taken in by the hypocritical question. Certainly Jesus was not fooled by the false solicitude of his enemies. It is interesting that Mark uses the same word for Christ's temptation in the desert. The Pharisees, like the devil, are trying to work against Jesus. His reproof to them is a quick recognition of their duplicity before he moves to demolishing their plan of a trap with the question that follows this one.

What can the question mean for us? I don't think that we should see it as something that could never apply to us in any way. If the Lord could call St. Peter "Satan" for disagreeing about the suffering that Jesus would have to endure, why could he not ask us, "Why are you putting me to the test?"

The scandalous French poet Charles Baudelaire wrote a note to the reader in his famous *Les Fleurs du Mal*. He addressed his future reader in this way: "Hypocrite reader, my double, my brother." Many of us try to pretend to be what we are not. We are actors in a script that we invent as we go along. Perhaps what we need to do is to place ourselves in the position of the Pharisees and Herodians. Don't we have some encounters with the Lord in which we are not completely sincere?

If Jesus thought that his disciples were in danger of their "leaven," aren't we also? What about our hypocrisy? We may not oppose Jesus or put traps for him, but we pretend sometimes to sincerely seek his will when we are really only convinced in the necessity of seeking what our own wills prompt us to seek.

This is often obvious in our prayer. In the Old Testament, the priest Eli, realizing that God has called out to Samuel a third time, tells the young prophet to respond the next time around to the voice of God by saying, "Speak, LORD, for thy servant hears" (1 Samuel 3:9). The way this works out in practice, it would often be more honest for us to say, "Listen, Lord, for your servant speaks." We pretend to want to know what the Lord wants, we are "discerning," but we really don't want to hear something unexpected. Are we putting the Lord to the test? ◇

"Whose likeness and inscription is this?"   — Mark 12:16

I cannot help but think that, as clever as this response to the question about the imperial taxes was, it did not save Jesus' life. It should have, because he very clearly demonstrates here that he was not what he was executed as, which was as a rebel against Roman authority. And yet, when he died, the Roman soldiers placed on his cross a sign in three languages that said, "Jesus of Nazareth, King of the Jews." We should not forget that the familiar *INRI* we know from so many representations of the crucifixion is a political note. The first "official" version of his death cast the Savior as an enemy of the Roman Empire, a pretender to the no-longer-existent throne of the no-longer-existent Jewish State.

An English atheist once said that it would be very difficult to persuade a modern judge of the truth of the Resurrection. The great English writer G. K. Chesterton responded, "It does not seem to occur to him that we Christians may not have such an extravagant reverence for English judges [as he feels]. The experiences of the Founder of Christianity have perhaps left us in a vague doubt of the infallibility of courts of law" ("The Blatchford Controversies," in *The Collected Works of G. K. Chesterton, Vol. I: Heretics, Orthodoxy, Blatchford Controversies*, Ignatius Press, 1986).

Perhaps they leave a vague doubt about the infallibility of the State, too. Many have used this answer of Jesus about Caesar's image on the coin to propose the legitimacy of the State and secular authority. The autonomy of the secular, the "two swords" theory, the separation of Church and State — all have been presented as somehow related to Jesus' ironic question. This might be making more of the answer than the clever lobby back to the court of the opponents that it was.

The feigned innocence implied in this question is noteworthy. It is clear that the Lord would have to know whose image and inscription were on the common coin. "You carry the man's coins," he is saying; "pay him his taxes." If anything, Jesus seems to be indicating a studied nonchalance about the secular order. It is of only relative importance, Jesus is saying, which is an obvious conclusion to the ironic question. In this it resembles the withering response to Pilate's somewhat petulant claim to power, "You would have no power over me unless it had been given you from above" (John 19:11).

What Jesus is really clarifying here is that his authority has nothing in common with that of the State. One of the most important lessons of the century just past for the Christian ought to be that the State can be a frightful thing. The Fascist dictator of Italy, Benito Mussolini, expressed frankly the theory of the totalitarian State when he said, "Everything within the State, nothing outside the State, nothing against the State." The twentieth century was the era *par excellence* of the power of Caesar. The deaths for which Communism, Nazism, and the various ideologies and nationalisms were responsible during the last one hundred years are numbers so fantastic as to numb the imagination. As one of the great masters of the murderous State, Joseph Stalin, pointed out, "One death is a tragedy, a million deaths are a statistic."

One way to interpret Jesus' answer is that he is pointing out his powerlessness in comparison with the great sociopolitical and socioeconomic system that was the Roman Empire. The great lesson of Caesar's coin is that God, the source of all power, chose to be powerless. The real power of God, to speak the language of paradox to which we are almost always reduced when talking about the Divine, is his powerlessness. The French preacher Bossuet encapsulated this when he said, "The crown of our monarch is made of thorns." Jesus is saying that God is not something measured by taxes or the power to impose them.

God is marginal in terms of what the Herodians and Pharisees were interested in.

But, of course we have the testimony of St. Paul, who received the revelation in 2 Corinthians 12:9, which tells us: "My power is made perfect in weakness." And in his response about the image of Tiberius Caesar on the coin lies the basis of an absolute claim upon us. The *Catena Aurea* quotes Pseudo-Jerome (for a time confused with St. Jerome, the great Bible translator and commentator) about the real message of Jesus to the Pharisees and Herodians. If the one whose image was stamped on a coin was in some way its owner, then what about man, who is made in the image and likeness of God? To paraphrase Mark 12:17, "Render to Caesar the money bearing his image, which is collected for him, and render yourselves willingly to God, for the light of your countenance, O Lord, and not of Caesar's, is stamped upon us."

A friend of mine told his congregation about the division of labor between his parents when he was a child. His mother handled the day-to-day decisions: where they lived and what they would eat and how they would occupy their time. On the other hand, his father was in charge of 'the big picture," for example, "Whether Red China should get a seat in the U.N. or not." There was a comic disproportion about which questions were really important for the life of the family.

Jesus is perhaps contrasting here the all-importance of what we owe God with the relative importance of the political order. What we owe God is both transcendent and immanent, with the most far-reaching consequences and the most practical demands. The question for us has to be what we see as really important. Do we give to God what is his?

Isn't everything his?

St. Ignatius Loyola, the founder of the Jesuit order of Roman Catholic priests, made a prayer that can serve us as a personal response to the command to give to God what is God's.

Receive, Lord, my liberty, my memory, my understanding, my entire will. All that I have and possess, You gave me, and I return it to You as Yours. I give it over to You entirely, to be governed by Your Will. Give me only Your Love and Your Grace, they are riches enough for me, and I can ask for nothing more. Amen.

It is a prayer worth meditating. ◇

"Is not this why you are wrong, that you know neither the scriptures nor the power of God?"   — Mark 12:24

Even out of context, this question has much to say to us. Isn't the criticism of us exactly right, that we neither know the Scripture as we ought nor do we recognize the real power of God? Isn't it obvious that we live in a time with little faith?

This question is addressed to the Sadducees. They were an elite group of Jews, an aristocracy, a curious religious aristocracy that was skeptical about the spiritual. They denied the immortality of the soul, and thus the possibility of resurrection, as well as the existence of spiritual beings, like angels and devils. Their name probably comes from Zadoc, the high priest whose priestly line was considered legitimate because he had served in the time of David.

They were priestly dynastic families, both wealthy and politically powerful. Maybe this life was enough for them, since they were well satisfied with it. Josephus, in his writings in Greek explaining Judaism to the Roman world, compared them to the Epicureans, the philosophic school that sought a minimum of pain in life. The Epicurean ideal was not hedonistic because it was not based on excessive pleasures of the senses but neither was it altruistic. The Sadducees obeyed the Torah and all the specific laws of the Old Testament. However, their perspective on life was strictly secular — there was no other life but this one. Although the New Testament does not highlight their role in opposition to Jesus as much as it does that of the Pharisees, it is clear that the Sadducees bore political responsibility for the death of Jesus.

Their question to Jesus, to which he has typically answered with a question, was about a far-fetched case of a widow who had married seven brothers in pursuit of an heir. Deuteronomy 25:5-10 outlines the legal background. The so-called "levirate law" declared that a man who lived in the same house as his brother could marry the widow on the latter's demise, with the condition that the first son born to the new couple would be considered the child of the dead brother. The law contemplates a ritual insult: spitting in the face and giving the nickname "shoeless" to any brother who would refuse to give an heir to his sibling and guarantee the welfare of his widow.

The Sadducees imagine seven brothers and the same bride. The comic exaggeration (after a few brothers died, you'd think the current husband would order food from outside the house, at least) is intentional, and is probably why Jesus responds a bit curtly. The Sadducees are mocking belief in the afterlife. He cites the Torah to them because it was the only part of the Jewish Scriptures (what we call the Old Testament) that they believed to be inspired. If God said to Moses that he was the God of Abraham, Isaac, and Jacob, how could those men be nonexistent? If they had died, and disappeared from being, why would God bother to mention them?

The argument sounds rabbinical in its dependence on a citation read from a very particular point of view. Nevertheless, it contains an essential teaching of faith. Our God does not just let us die but invites us to another life. We could put in many other names where Jesus puts the fathers of the people of Israel. We could say, "God of my father, my grandmother, my aunt, my husband, my brother, my sister, my son, my daughter." Our God is the God of the living because, for him, all are alive.

While I was writing this reflection, something curious happened to me. I got stuck about halfway through and decided that the Lord "gives to his beloved sleep," as it says in Psalm

127:2. Before I woke up, I dreamed of an aunt who was very special to me. She has been dead now several years, and, in fact, I was present when she breathed her last breath. Nevertheless, in the dream I acted surprised not to have seen her. I told her that I missed her and I had the sensation of weeping just before I awoke.

Part of Jesus' question answering the question of the Sadducees involves the mystery of what life will be like after death. The trick question of the Sadducees — "Whose wife will she be when the resurrection occurs?" (cf. Mark 12:23) — was based upon the premise that eternal life is just the continuation of the present life. Many fantasies of heaven are handicapped by the failure to accept that the other life will be a transformation of this one.

Julian Barnes, the English novelist, has a wicked story that presents heaven as a perpetual wish fulfillment that ends up being worse than hell. The person who goes to heaven eventually realizes that it is boring to score thirty-six playing golf on thirty-six holes and always succeeding at whatever activity one's involved in. I presume that the story is meant to mock belief in the afterlife. Actually, it is a useful parable for a believer. The new life we will have in Christ will be a life like that of the angels (cf. Mark 12:25), a life that will transcend so many of our categories.

A seminary teacher once told us that we should think of eternal life in terms of this comparison. The child within the womb has a human existence. He or she can hear music, apparently, and is sensitive to touch. In fact, the still unborn can react to danger sensed entirely through his or her mother. Then the child's world is destroyed and he or she is thrown into what must seem the cruel light of a new and extraordinarily different world. The difference of existence between unborn and born life, said the teacher, is minor in comparison to that between life before and after death. As the unborn child could not suspect what awaits him or her, neither can we anticipate all the changes that will take place in us after death.

We will not be married, said Jesus to the Sadducees. We might wish that he would have expatiated on the topic. How will our life be? That is something we will have to wait until the day "when we will have no more questions" (cf. Matthew 22:46, Mark 12:34, Luke 20:40). ◇

"How can the scribes say that the Christ is the son of David? David himself, inspired by the Holy Spirit, declared, / 'The Lord said to my Lord, / Sit at my right hand, / till I put thy enemies under thy feet.' / David himself calls him Lord; so how is he his son?"   — Mark 12:35-37

Jesus asks these questions of the "great throng" that is listening to him teach in the Temple. They frame a kind of syllogism, a logical structure that has two premises lead to a conclusion. In this example the premises are:

   1. "The scribes say that the Christ is the son of David."
   2. But David calls the Christ "my Lord."
   Therefore, the scribes are not correct.

This is a little confusing in the context of the New Testament, because Jesus' connection with David seems to be insisted upon in other places, especially in the Gospels of Matthew and Luke, which describe the birth of Jesus in Bethlehem and give detailed genealogies proving Davidic descent. In Mark 2:25-28, Jesus mentions with approval that David broke ritual law eating the bread of offering and implies some association with the king because he concludes, "so the Son of man is lord even of the sabbath." The connection is more explicit in the story of the blind Bartimaeus in chapter 10, verses 46-52. The blind man of Jericho shouts: "Jesus, Son of David, have mercy on me!" (Mark 10:47). Jesus does not object to being called this and on the contrary calls the man over and asks him, "What do you want me to do for you?" (Mark 10:51). Surely, if Jesus resented the title "Son of David," he could have made that clear at that point.

In order to respect the insistence in St. Luke and St. Matthew on the Davidic descent of Jesus, we have to take a closer look at what Jesus is saying. One important clarification is of the term "the Christ," which translates the Greek *Christos* here. *Christos* is literally "the Anointed," and is used as the standard translation of the Hebrew *Messiah*.

Perhaps we need to see Jesus' question more as, "*How* is the Messiah the son of David?" The answer is complicated. The Christ is the eternal Son of God and the king's Lord, but he is also David's son. The *how* of the second question reaches to the mystery of "God made man" in Jesus. The scribes were interpreting the title "Son of David" as something that limited the Messiah. It meant that the Messiah was not divine. For the scribes and Pharisees the scandal of Jesus' ministry was his insistence on his divinity. That is why his forgiveness of sin troubled them so much.

I suppose that some of the critics of Jesus sincerely thought that the promised Messiah had to be one who brought about political liberation. For more than ten years of my life I have lived in El Salvador, and not infrequently I have heard from even church people that a Jesus who had nothing to do with the political liberation of the people (and that often very narrowly defined as vague left-wing politics, friendly to the political tyranny in Cuba) was not the real one. Obviously, belief in Jesus has to mean dedication to justice. It also means a commitment to the civilization of love. However, a theology that tolerates political violence or weds itself to one single system seems very limited to me. Jesus taught us something that should transform politics but definitely transcends it. David the king, in this prophetic psalm, saw Jesus and called him Lord, not his political heir. If Jesus offered us only political liberation, would he command our hearts?

Jesus worked a revolution in world history but was not a revolutionary in the sense of one interested in political power and strategies. Christian faith must always avoid the extremes of political entanglement and a flight from this world and its problems. We are in the world to transform it, and that transformation is the start of that real dream which Jesus called his kingdom. However, the Savior does not have a specific political program. He means to save us from sin and all its sad and selfish corollaries.

Our own commitment to Jesus means being able to understand this question. Although few North Americans see him primarily as a political figure, many have trouble seeing him as Lord in more than a politely perfunctory sense of the word.

St. Mark says that "the great throng heard him [Jesus] gladly" (Mark 12:37). Their joy was a sign of independence of the religious establishment, but it was apparently a momentary thing. They would soon demonstrate that they had no special loyalty to Jesus. It was a "throng" that shouted for the release of Barabbas instead of Jesus only a few days after this incident in the Temple.

Couldn't we be in the position of that throng? We claim to know that the Messiah was both the son of David and much more than his son. However, how do we show that? Psalm 110, which talks about the king who is also the priest, tells us about our Messiah, Christ the Lord. He rules us and sanctifies us. Jesus' question to the crowd was about why others misinterpreted him. Perhaps he would ask us now why we do not see his absolute claims over us. ◇

"Do you see these great buildings? There will not be left here one stone upon another, that will not be thrown down."

— Mark 13:2

In St. Mark, there is an inescapable sensation that the apostles of Jesus were rubes. They pick grains on the Sabbath and pop them in their mouths. They forget to wash their hands before they eat. They are also awfully impressed with the construction of Herod's Temple. This question of Jesus is a response to their admiration for the Temple and is another example of how the Lord did not attempt to be subtle when he wanted to redirect his disciples' attention.

According to Josephus, the Temple in Jerusalem was indeed a wonder of the world. He says, "Of its stones, some of them were forty-five cubits in length, five in height and six in breadth" (*Daily Study Bible for the New Testament: Gospel of Mark*, by William Barclay, Westminster John Knox Press, 1975). A cubit, says Webster, is an ancient measure of between eighteen and twenty-two inches of length. I suppose we all might be impressed by a building with such elements, even though we are not fishermen from Galilee.

We can relate to this question when we think of the World Trade Center Towers in New York. Most of us have etched in our minds a picture of the buildings towering above the New York City skyline as well as the image of those towers — with nearly three thousand doomed souls in them — falling and being reduced to rubble.

Jesus really asks us, by means of this question, whether we will continue to be impressed by works that are of their nature temporary. If the disciples could have seen into the future, they would have beheld a Temple mount totally destroyed by Roman troops punishing the rebellious Jews who rose up against the Empire in A.D. 69.

The so-called Wailing Wall is not an exception to this prophecy. It is really only the remains of a retaining wall built to extend Mount Moriah for the tremendous platform on which Herod's Temple rested. Of the glory of Herod's work, which included plates of gold on the front, only a few stones of a part of its foundation can be seen today. There pious Jews weep for their lost Temple, and some tourists imitate their prayer by writing on bits of paper and stuffing them in the cracks of the old stones.

The history of the Temple reminds us of Shelley's poem "Ozymandias." In it a traveler recounts seeing pieces of an enormous statue in the desert, the pedestal of which bears this legend:

> "My name is Ozymandias, king of kings:
> Look on my works, ye Mighty, and despair!"
> Nothing beside remains. Round the decay
> Of that colossal wreck, boundless and bare
> The lone and level sands stretch far away.

Human works are not made to last. We ought to think of what most impresses us in human achievement. Inevitably, we must say, "This, too, must pass." Sometimes our admiration is more subtly expressed than that of the apostles, but it is often just as misplaced. One day the lone and level sands will surround what we think is something as secure as the people of Jesus' day considered the Temple.

There is more here than a prediction of the Jewish revolt against Rome and its awful consequences, however. Jesus is not merely saying that nothing will endure. He identified himself with the Temple. One of the accusations against him when the Sanhedrin met on the night before he died was that he had said, "I will destroy this temple that is made with hands, and in three days I will build another, not made with hands" (Mark 14:58). St. John has Jesus say exactly that at the time of the cleansing of the Temple (cf. John 2:19). His listeners object that Herod's Temple had been in construction for forty-six years. The evangelist clarifies: "But he was speaking of the temple of his own body" (cf. John 2:21).

The Temple was the place of encounter with God. Jesus was saying he himself was the new venue for the experience of God. Not stones and mortar but flesh and blood had become the point of communion with the Divine. The Temple of Jerusalem was destroyed but never to be built again. The temple of his body was destroyed but was raised again. In Jesus, Nature's cycle of destruction and new beginning is perfectly transformed. In Greek myth, the Phoenix burned its nest in order to be born again; however, its renewal was not transcendence but repetition. It was starting over again on a closed circuit.

Jesus' Resurrection is a new beginning that is not a repetition. It is entering on another plane; it is not just a renewal of a lease. We are not chained to repeating what has happened, like the Greek Sisyphus who never reaches the top of the hill with the great stone he is pushing. In Jesus we can move beyond ourselves to a new creation.

One of the constants of human endeavor has been the seeking of immortality. Kings wanted to conquer it, poets celebrate it, and families guarantee it. So many plans of mice and men have gone awry. That is why it would do us some good to listen to Jesus in this exchange. I imagine him looking with a somber eye at the great walls of the Temple. Who could have understood more the almost infinite details of the effort it represented, from the regal pride that was its commencement to the sweat of the lowliest slave carrying water for the work? I think about how I watch ants scurry to rebuild an anthill a careless step has destroyed. So much feverish activity and so little duration.

Jesus asks me about the things I admire, "Do you see these great works?" I need to hear him say, "Not a stone upon a stone." May his words make me think of what is really of lasting importance. ◇

"Let her alone; why do you trouble her?"   — Mark 14:6

This question of Jesus is about the woman who anointed his head with very expensive perfume. Because we are interested here only in St. Mark, we cannot pretend to know more about the woman than we find here. A natural temptation is to blend her with the woman in St. Luke who anoints Christ's feet with perfume and is explicitly "forgiven, for she loved much" (Luke 7:47). Mark is not interested in the theme of repentance here, as Luke was in the story in that Gospel. What interests our evangelist is the extravagance of the gesture. He is preoccupied about the expense of the perfume and how that squares with the preaching of the kingdom.

In his nervousness about the luxury implied in the anointing, he seems to leave out some details and almost contradicts himself. He says that "some" were angry about the gesture and "said to themselves" that the perfume should have been sold for the poor. Despite the fact that their anger was something "interior," they externalize it promptly by beginning to reproach the woman. Their criticism does not sound like it comes from the host, the mysterious Simon the Leper. In fact, the supposed concern for the poor sounds more like Jesus himself, who preached the kingdom of the poor.

St. Matthew frankly says that the critics are the disciples (cf. Matthew 26:8). St. John, in a passage that is parallel, mentions Judas Iscariot (cf. John 12:4). Nevertheless, we can conclude that Mark knows that the ones with the problem are the disciples. Surely Jesus would not answer critics who were on the outside of his movement that "wherever the gospel is preached in the whole world, what she has done will be told in memory of her" (Mark 14:9). This would not impress people who were not followers. Jesus here is letting his followers know that their first reaction to this incident was erroneous.

It is easy to understand the objection of the disciples. The perfume, which came all the way from India in the time of Jesus, was extremely expensive. Can you imagine something similar, costing three hundred days' wages in the United States, used up in a single throw? How would that play today within the Church?

Christ himself seems to sense an objection to the woman's gesture, because he hastens to say in her defense that "you always have the poor with you" (Matthew 26:11, Mark 14:7; cf. John 12:8). In my opinion the incautious use of this citation has justified more than a few sins against solidarity, although who am I to judge such things? An important detail to keep in mind with regard to this saying is that the Lord is actually citing Scripture: "The poor will never cease out of the land; therefore I command you, You shall open wide your hand to your brother, to the needy and to the poor, in the land" (Deuteronomy 15:11).

What the woman does, says Jesus, is something "beautiful." This seems strange. We are used to Jesus teaching about something "good" — but something "beautiful"? The Greek words are actually used interchangeably several times in the New Testament, but it still sounds like aesthetics where we are expecting ethics. Its aestheticism combines oddly with a concept of fame, which also seems surprising in the Gospel. *Sub specie aeternitatis*, "according to eternal categories" — what difference does it make that the woman would be mentioned wherever the Gospel be told? Is not this still a human fame?

Obviously Jesus is not arguing that the fame of the woman's gesture (not her fame, personally, because we are not even given a name for her) is a justification of her deed. He must be saying that the symbolic largesse of what she did is essentially related to the Good News. How can that be?

Perhaps he is telling us that we have to be careful about our judgment of other disciples. His followers wanted to reproach her for what she did. It is interesting that they did not attempt to raise an objection directly with him. Was this because they did not understand that he would soon die, and any gesture of tenderness toward him would be made much more important to them? Or was it because there was a dangerous pragmatism in their attitude even toward Jesus? Was their commitment to the kingdom ideological, rather than based upon personal faith? Certainly, one could conclude from the anointing incident in St. John that Judas had turned against Christ in part because of Jesus' tolerance of the woman's extreme devotion. St. Mark does not make this explicit but does connect Judas's betrayal sequentially.

The anointing was an anticipation of Christ's burial. Can transcendence be calculated in days' wages? It makes me wonder: Do we trouble people who perhaps seem to sin against our own narrow categories of what should or should not be done in discipleship? Do we forget that the life of transcendence is beyond material categories?

I wonder if Mother Teresa of Calcutta was inspired by this passage to say she wanted to do "something beautiful for God." For some people, her life had its own kind of extravagance. This had nothing to do with luxuries, of course. When she was given the Nobel Peace Prize in 1979, she asked that the money that might have been spent on the grand banquet traditionally offered the winner be given to the poor instead. But in other ways, she sometimes offended people's ideas about practicality and refused to think merely in terms of dollars and cents, especially with regard to abortion. She would not accept that economic scarcity would justify the death of the innocent.

Her ideas of religious life were not considered by all to be the best for our day. I heard her say once that even she had doubts about part of the rule of her order. She said that when her sisters asked that a holy hour before the Blessed Sacrament be added to each day's tasks, she had been opposed. "How will we get all our work done?" she had asked the chapter. The sisters had been adamant, however, and she acceded, for which she was grateful afterward.

Some really great leaders in Christianity have been the opposite of pragmatic. Their devotion caused them to use up the perfume of their talent for *beaux gestes* that others did not understand. People wondered about so much energy for what at times seemed marginal. Nevertheless, beauty has a way of triumphing over pragmatism. Perhaps that is why this question should echo in our ears. If we had been there, would we have troubled the woman? Are we troubling someone now who is doing a necessary sacrifice? ⟨⟩

"Simon, are you asleep? Could you not watch one hour?"
— Mark 14:37

Three times in the Gospel of St. Mark Jesus shows a prefer-
ence for the company of Peter, James, and John, making
them a kind of inner circle within the inner circle of the twelve
apostles. The first time is in Mark 5:37, when the Lord allows
only the three of them to follow him to Jairus's house after
reports that the man's daughter has died. The second time is at
the Transfiguration on Mount Tabor (cf. Mark 9:2). The third
time is here in the garden of Gethsemani. The first time was to
witness the Lord's power over life, the second time to have a
glimpse of his glory, and the third time to accompany him in
his agony and see how much he hurt.

Of the three, Peter, of course, has the highest profile in the
New Testament. Perhaps that is why this question of Jesus is
addressed to him specifically, although the other disciples are
also sleeping. There might be here a hint of the Lord trying to
make Peter more humble. It was Peter, who, only a little while
before, had said, "Even though they all fall away, I will not"
(Mark 14:29). Jesus had told him after that remark that he would
soon deny him three times. Here he asks him, if we take a look
at the Greek, "Were you not *strong* enough to watch one hour?"

The idea of strength comes from the Greek verb used here,
ischyo, which can mean, "to be strong," "to be capable of something," "to be powerful." Peter, the one who had asserted himself as stronger than the others at the Last Supper, was not
strong enough to stay awake for an hour. The love between
Jesus and Peter had to be very deep to withstand Peter's weakness on one side and the Lord's tremendously ironic honesty

on the other. "So here is the strong one" is what this question implies: "How are you better than the others?" We can imagine Peter at least discomfited by this, if not altogether abashed at his own debility, his human weakness. After all, Peter was a fisherman and often had had to stay up at night working. It was not something far out of his reach to await the dawn. The poor fishermen who work the Pacific coast here in El Salvador are used to losing sleep.

But the situation of the disciples is not just an anecdote from the last hours of the Lord's life. It is clear that the situation of the disciples and their part in the agony in the garden has great symbolic ramifications. There is much more to the story than sleepy friends. The moment offers a kind of model of the dangers of discipleship. The friends of the Lord can grow sleepy, even when he tells them that it is necessary to "watch and pray." They (and we) can be indifferent to what the Lord is suffering and can lose themselves (and ourselves) in sleep.

St. Thomas More noted this when he drew out a contrast between Peter, James, and John and Judas Iscariot: "Judas the traitor at the same time was so wide awake and intent on betraying the Lord that the very idea of sleep never entered his mind. Does not this contrast between the traitor and the apostles present to us a clear and sharp mirror image (as it were), a sad and terrible view of what has happened through the ages from those times even to our own?" The good are "sleepy and apathetic" said the English martyr, while the "enemies of Christ . . . are wide awake — so much wiser (as Christ says) are the sons of darkness in their generation than the sons of light" (*The Navarre Bible: St. Mark's Gospel*, Four Courts Press, 1992).

This ingenious comparison recalls the famous lines from "The Second Coming," a poem by W. B. Yeats: "The best lack all conviction, while the worst / Are full of passionate intensity."

We might want to make a personal application here. A priest friend of mine used to say, "I resemble that remark" instead of "I resent that remark." Perhaps we resemble Yeats's remark about lacking conviction. Where is our passionate intensity? What can keep us from sleeping?

The word that Jesus uses here for staying awake is used other times in the New Testament to mean more than not sleeping. It has a figurative sense of being vigilant and is connected with the themes of judgment and the Second Coming. There is a curious doubling effect in the text right after this question. "You could not stay awake? / Stay awake!" is another possible translation.

There is a science-fiction horror film called *The Invasion of the Body Snatchers*. When I saw the original version as a boy, I remember being impressed by the problem of the heroes. My recall of the details is a bit vague, but the premise was that the characters in the movie would be taken over by aliens if they fell asleep. The unconscious brain would surrender to the snatchers. At least in the way I recall it, the situation seems like a perfect nightmare. How could they stay awake so that the monsters could not take over?

When I saw it, I had not studied the Bible. I did not know the word *eschaton*, the Greek word for "the end of the world." From *eschaton* comes the word *eschatological*, which means having to do with the Second Coming. Nevertheless, the movie could be a good parable of the vigilance required for the *eschaton*. If we fall asleep, we are lost. The imagery is very biblical and has to do with the warnings of vigilance that always accompany teaching about the end of this world in the New Testament.

The message is not just to the three who were sleeping in the garden. We are all expected to be strong enough to watch "an hour." We are all to be cognizant of the challenge revealed in the words Jesus says to Peter immediately after this question, "The spirit indeed is willing, but the flesh is weak" (Mark 14:38).

That is why we should all substitute our own names for that of Simon Peter. Many who make holy hours before the

Blessed Sacrament have felt these words echo in their consciousness. In that moment he wanted Peter to accompany him in his prayer. In this moment he wants my company. The question for me becomes: "Richard, are you strong enough to watch and pray?"

Substitute your name for mine, dear reader, since the question is for you, too. ◇

"Are you still sleeping and taking your rest?" — Mark 14:41

This "question" is really a question of translation. The words for "sleeping" and "taking rest" are in the imperative, not in the interrogative, form in the original Greek. Many different translators have grappled with this grammar and have decided that it makes more sense to have Jesus ask a question than to give an order. There is a manuscript source that supports this variation, and so this citation gives us a glimpse of the scholarly shadows projected by some texts.

If it is a question, Jesus is repeating himself to intensify the message. In fact, this is a triple event, something common in folk tales (remember the three wishes on Aladdin's lamp) and in the Bible (three times St. Peter denies Jesus, three times the resurrected Jesus asks St. Peter, "Do you love me?"). Three times Jesus interrupts his prayer to see whether the disciples are still praying. The first time he addresses himself to Simon. The second time, Mark does not report what Jesus says, but he does say of the disciples that he found them sleeping "and they did not know what to answer him" (Mark 14:40). The third intervention is also addressed to the three disciples.

Three strikes and you're out. The proverbial expression certainly comes to mind in the case of Peter in the courtyard of the high priest's residence, and it serves to remind us here of God's mercy. Three strikes and you're not out altogether. In the question form, Jesus' words can echo in our own ears and make us want to change. Am I still sleeping? How many times must the Lord come to me to ask me to accompany him in his agony before I consent to join him in prayer?

For that is the really surprising truth of this incident in the garden. Jesus could not take being completely alone with the immensity of alienation he was to swallow in the cup offered him by his Father. It is a revealing view of Jesus we receive in this pericope of Scripture. He is feeling desperate and wants some company in his prayer. William Barclay, the Scottish Scripture commentator, says of this part of St. Mark: "This is a passage we almost fear to read, for it seems to intrude into the private agony of Jesus" (*Daily Study Bible for the New Testament: Gospel of Mark*, by William Barclay, Westminster John Knox Press, 1975).

It is obvious that we must identify ourselves and our myriad petty failings with the sleeping disciples. No doubt they were tired, with a fatigue that the tension of the moment exacerbates in many of us. Their eyelids would not stay open. They submerged themselves in sleep.

Shakespeare has one of literature's great insomniacs, Macbeth, comment on nocturnal rest in words that are well remembered:

> Sleep that knits up the ravell'd sleave of care,
> The death of each day's life, sore labour's bath,
> Balm of hurt minds, great nature's second course,
> Chief nourisher in life's feast.

Lady Macbeth had spoken with less attractiveness when she had pointed out that when the king's servants turned in, "in swinish sleep, / Their drenched natures lie as in death" thus permitting her evil plan, "What cannot you and I perform upon / The unguarded Duncan?" Jesus had confided in his disciples that he would be searched for, and so their vigilance would have been not only spiritually but also corporally prudent. However, they were overcome with sleep. Certainly Jesus would be justified in feeling frustrated with his disciples. How could they sleep at a time like this?

We must identify ourselves with Jesus at this critical moment. Many of us have known loneliness or can imagine it. How painful it is to be alone in suffering, especially spiritual suffering. Jesus was wrestling in that moment with the sin of the whole world. His disciples lose themselves in the inevitable solipsism of sleep. They could not "watch one hour" with him.

That is what makes possible the other reading of Jesus' words. Was he giving his sleeping disciples an ironic command, "Go ahead, sleep, take your rest"? Sarcasm and irony are not unknown in the Bible. Was Jesus being sarcastic here? Was he saying that it was useless for him to have asked them to watch and pray with him?

A sarcastic Jesus is frightening, although most of us could use a scare from time to time to shake us from our spiritual complacency. I think that Jesus was not asking a question here, but I imagine him practically whispering the words over the sleeping disciples. In my reading he is taking the measure of their weakness and wishes that they could "take their rest." Perhaps he was afraid for them. Perhaps he was humanly preoccupied about how they would fare without him. Both the weakness of these three special disciples and the consciousness of the great test that awaited them must have been present in the Lord's thoughts. Perhaps his annoyance with their failure in this instance gave way to a feeling of tenderness.

Like so many parts of Scripture, this passage invites us to enter what is described in our own imagination. Whether Jesus is questioning ironically or ordering sarcastically, the important thing is to see how his words might have application to us.

Do you ask me, Jesus, whether I am still sleeping? Do you mock my weakness telling me to sleep on? Hearing your voice has to awaken me, and I have to feel the force of your words, "The hour has come; the Son of man is betrayed into the hands of sinners" (Mark 14:41). ◇

"Have you come out as against a robber, with swords and clubs to capture me?"   — Mark 14:48

This question is addressed to the crowd who came to arrest Jesus in the garden of Gethsemani. The crowd included Judas, one of the twelve apostles, and others who are described as being "from the chief priests and the scribes and the elders" (Mark 14:43). The interrogative is rhetorical, like so many of the questions of Jesus, because the answer is obvious. Of course they have come out prepared for violence. Jesus wants to make them look at what they are doing, to be aware of how they look, to make them self-conscious about their own actions.

What did the Temple guards and hangers-on in the crowd think about what they were doing? Could they have felt that Jesus was dangerous enough to warrant the swords and clubs?

Some days before, Jesus had made a whip and driven the moneychangers and the vendors of animals for sacrifice from the Temple precincts. He had said at that time that the Temple authorities were thieves, that they had made the House of God into a robbers' den. Now they were after him as though he were the robber and not they.

I wonder how an ordinary Temple guard felt about this assignment. In the country where I live there are often armed guards in front of businesses. The first time I went to a fast-food place in San Salvador, I was surprised to see a man with a rifle in front. Later, I became accustomed to the many private policemen and usually I greet them. For them, it is a job, something that lets them put food on their table.

Were there some among the armed guards who were just doing their job? I do not doubt it. That does not make what was done explainable, let alone justifiable, but it does touch the mystery of evil. Elie Wiesel, the 1986 Nobel Peace Prize winner who survived Auschwitz, once wrote that not all the guards who were involved in the extermination policy of the Third Reich hated the Jews. In fact, many seemed not to hate the Jewish children they were killing. And that, he said, was even more frightening, that a person could do such abominable injustice *without* hate. Participation in evil seems sometimes inevitable, as if a person had stepped into some quicksand that sucks him in and his every effort makes him sink deeper. Think of how many people have compromised themselves by participation in some way with the plague of abortion in our society. Many of them might even say that they are *personally* opposed to it but that their job or our constitution requires them to tolerate some things.

Jesus pointed out to the mob that they had seen him teaching in the Temple every day. I am sure that the normal reaction to his pointing this out would be shame. In the Gospel of John the crowd falls prostrate when Jesus identifies himself in Gethsemani. There must have been some doubt in the ordinary people who had seen Jesus around the Temple. They must have felt the power of this man, something that had been revealed when he scribbled in the dirt and made the homicidal crowd let the adulterous woman go free. The swords and clubs were for themselves, and for their own fears, not because of Jesus. How did these men feel after Jesus was crucified?

Someone was there who had to feel even guiltier. He had just greeted his Master with a kiss. He knew more than anyone that Jesus was not a thief. Although there is some discussion about whether Judas Iscariot intended the death of Jesus, I don't see how he could not have seen from the garden that this was going to be a criminal procedure. Just a little bit further in the Gospel, Jesus' question becomes a kind of prophecy fulfilled in this verse, "And with him they crucified two robbers, one on his right and one on his left" (Mark 15:27).

They came to arrest him as though for a robber and they executed him likewise. What had Judas Iscariot wanted? The end result was that his "Master" was killed as a criminal. The personal rejection of the discipleship of Jesus that Judas had effected by going to the chief priests to sell out his Master had set off a chain of events that ended in violence. Although St. Mark does not mention this question of Jesus, St. Luke does: "Judas, would you betray the Son of man with a kiss?" (Luke 22:48). Matthew has still another version, "Friend, why are you here?" (Matthew 26:50).

Despite the fact that Mark does not report the direct question to Judas, this one had to echo a bit in his mind. As it should in our minds. We will not be judged as were the Temple guards, who very likely did not realize what was going on. We will be judged like Judas, as those who have been given some intimacy with the Lord and yet sometimes betray him. The rhetorical objection to the violence of his captors was really another way of saying, "What do you take me for?" This might have provoked shame for the cowardice of not arresting him in the Temple. Or it might have had to do with the intuition that Jesus was obviously a holy man, and therefore it was shameful to treat him as a man of violence. But for Judas this was a question about the identity of Jesus and his own relationship to him.

The Byzantine Catholic liturgy has a prayer before communion that includes the wish "not to betray you with a kiss like Judas." I thought this strange the first few times I heard it. At the very moment when we are to enter into sacramental intimacy with the Lord, the liturgy was reminding us of betrayal. The more I have meditated on this, however, the more that I have seen the wisdom of recalling that intimacy can turn to betrayal. That is the story of marriages and love affairs, and it is also a truth about our own relationship with Christ. Our intimacy with the Lord needs to be purified with a self-conscious aversion of betraying him.

If we listened to this question with the ears of Judas, what changes would we want to make in our relationship with Jesus? ◇

And at the ninth hour Jesus cried out with a loud voice, "Eloi, Eloi, lama sabachthani?" which means, "My God, my God, why hast thou forsaken me?"   — Mark 15:34

A very pious old woman once told me a story about herself that surprised me. Some fifty years before, she had been a young mother with a sick husband. After work one evening she had been walking across a big bridge in Cleveland, Ohio. She was tired, and saw no hope for rest in sight. Her life was desperate and there was no one who could understand her. The dark shadows below the bridge, which crosses a river at a great height, seemed to call out to her.

She felt the temptation to jump off the side of the bridge. Because she had never been suicidal before, she was terrified at the idea taking control of her mind. The only sound she heard was that made by her own steps. A moment on the great concrete banister and then all would be over. Never had she felt so utterly alone. Never had she been able to forget everyone else in her life. Never had she been so close to death.

This story had a happy ending. She crossed the bridge and survived, although the temptation had some lingering force in her. Then she worked up the nerve to go to confession. Of course, she was afraid that the priest would be angry with her. What right did she have to think of taking her own life? She deliberately chose the younger priest's confessional line when she got to church.

"I told him, and he seemed to understand," she told me. "I never expected anyone to understand the terrible fear I had in me. But he really understood me. It made all the difference in the world to me. It changed how I saw everything. Somebody knew it was hard; somebody could see it."

I often think about that young priest. Was he acquainted with lonely suffering so well that he had been able to recognize the temptation to despair? Or had he conquered some similar trial? Perhaps his own background is not to the point, but I cannot help thinking that the lady was telling me about his compassion in the confessional to help me help others.

He had not been able to get her another job, nor cure her sick husband, nor see about her living conditions. He had simply been able to humanize her experience by letting her know that he understood what she was suffering. It had been more important to understand her than to suggest any changes. The crucial thing had been that she would know that she was not alone in her suffering, because someone else could understand it.

This question of Jesus is also about understanding what can be called the ultimate temptation — despair. Anyone who has felt abandoned by God can feel that Jesus was there, too. These words are among the seven last words of Christ (each word being a phrase). There can be no question that those who have felt the chill winds of despair in their souls can identify with Jesus on the cross, or better, that he could identify with them.

In the *Catena Aurea*, one of the writers, Theophylact, comments on what Christ expressed when he spoke about forsakenness: "He spoke therefore as a man, bearing about with him my feelings, for when placed in danger we fancy that we are deserted by God." There is a great consolation in these simple words: Jesus the Christ, the Son of God, was human and carried our feelings in his heart. The Church at the Second Vatican Council in the Constitution on the Church in the Modern World echoed the sentiments of the Roman playwright Terence, who said, *"Homo sum: humani nil a me alienum puto"* ("I am a man: I hold that nothing human is alien to me"). That is the great mystery of the Incarnation: Jesus, the Second Person of the Blessed Trinity, says, "Nothing human is alien to me."

I suppose that some might say that sin is alien to Jesus and that sin is human. Actually, sin is the corruption of humanity, not its essence. Besides this, Jesus took all the sins of the world upon himself. St. Paul said that God the Father "made him to be sin who knew no sin, so that in him we might become the righteousness of God" (2 Corinthians 5:21). Although sin was, of course, alien to Jesus, the mystical experience of sin was not. This is what made him sweat blood in Gethsemani and nailed him to the cross at Calvary. There are some commentators who say that the abandonment or forsakenness of Jesus was his probing of the vertiginous depths of sin, his recognition of the dark chasm of alienation that it opens between God and us.

There was a time when this question of Jesus was only a citation for me. I was afraid that people might be scandalized by the Lord, who sounded close to despair, and so I felt it necessary to emphasize the fact that the question is the first line of Psalm 22. Jesus was praying on the cross — I still try to think of that when I look at a crucifix — praying in Aramaic, his native tongue. The psalm, although dramatic in its first lines, safely concludes into a profession of confidence in the God of the poor.

Now I think, however, that it is no accident that the psalm is one that expresses forsakenness so well, nor that Jesus speaks only the first line. Gerard Manley Hopkins, the great English Jesuit poet, wrote in a sonnet on despair:

O the mind, mind has mountains; cliffs of fall
Frightful, sheer, no-man-fathomed. Hold them cheap
May who ne'er hung there.

Jesus hung there, on the cross. Anyone who has ever asked God a similar question, or wanted to, like the woman I wrote about above, knows what Jesus was talking about here. ◇

The Way
of Compassion

...into the heart of the
Seven Sorrows of Mary

Father Richard C. Antall

As a missionary in El Salvador, the author saw sorrow in its most tragic forms, sorrow brought on by the horrors of civil war. In these meditations of the Seven Sorrows of Mary, Father (now Monsignor) Antall tells the moving stories of seven women who, like Mary, endured great sorrow with great faith.
0-87973-854-5 (854), paper, 144 pp.

To order from Our Sunday Visitor:
Toll free: 1-800-348-2440
E-mail: osvbooks@osv.com
Website: www.osv.com

Availability of products subject to change without notice.

The author brings his experience in El Salvador's civil war to these profound and moving meditations on the Seven Last Words of Our Lord.
0-87973-340-3 (340), paper, 160 pp.

To order from Our Sunday Visitor:
Toll free: 1-800-348-2440
E-mail: osvbooks@osv.com
Website: www.osv.com

Availability of products subject to change without notice.

Patrick Madrid in his best-selling *Where Is That in Tradition?* shows the scriptural basis for often-questioned Catholic doctrines. Now he tackles the other half of the divine revelation with *Why Is That in Tradition?* When the Church is accused of adding man-made doctrinal aberrations that go against Scripture, this is the book to reach for.
1-931709-06-8 (T10), paper, 176 pp.

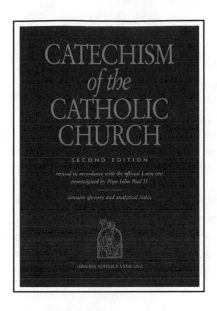

Here in one volume is the whole teaching of the Catholic Church, undiluted and uncompromised. The *Catechism* is not an *interpretation* of what Catholics believe; it *is* what Catholics believe. From animal experimentation to unemployment, it addresses all the most pressing moral questions of the modern world.
0-87973-976-2 (976), paper, 906 pp.
0-87973-977-0 (977), hardcover, 906 pp.

To order from Our Sunday Visitor:
Toll free: 1-800-348-2440
E-mail: osvbooks@osv.com
Website: www.osv.com

Availability of products subject to change without notice.

Our Sunday Visitor. . .
Your Source for Discovering the Riches of the Catholic Faith

Our Sunday Visitor has an extensive line of materials for young children, teens, and adults. Our books, Bibles, booklets, CD-ROMs, audios, and videos are available in bookstores worldwide.

To receive a FREE full-line catalog or for more information, call **Our Sunday Visitor** at **1-800-348-2440**. Or write, **Our Sunday Visitor** / 200 Noll Plaza / Huntington, IN 46750.

- -

Please send me: ___A catalog

Please send me materials on:

___Apologetics and catechetics   ___Reference works

___Prayer books   ___Heritage and the saints

___The family   ___The parish

Name_____

Address_____Apt._____

City_____State_____Zip_____

Telephone (   ) _____

A29BBABP

- -

Please send a friend: ___A catalog

Please send a friend materials on:

___Apologetics and catechetics   ___Reference works

___Prayer books   ___Heritage and the saints

___The family   ___The parish

Name_____

Address_____Apt._____

City_____State_____Zip_____

Telephone (   ) _____

A29BBABP

- -

Our Sunday Visitor
200 Noll Plaza
Huntington, IN 46750
Toll free: 1-800-348-2440
E-mail: osvbooks@osv.com
Website: www.osv.com